Linkedin

Guide to Making Your Linkedin Profile Awesome

(How to Build Relationships and Get Job Offers Using Linkedin)

Kevin McMahon

Published By **Phil Dawson**

Kevin McMahon

Linkedin: Guide to Making Your Linkedin Profile Awesome (How to Build Relationships and Get Job Offers Using Linkedin)

ISBN   978-1-998927-48-7

No part of this guidebook shall be reproduced in any form without permission in writing from the publisher except in the case of brief quotations embodied in critical articles or reviews.

Legal & Disclaimer

The information contained in this book is not designed to replace or take the place of any form of medicine or professional medical advice. The information in this book has been provided for educational & entertainment purposes only.

The information contained in this book has been compiled from sources deemed reliable, and it is accurate to the best of the Author's knowledge; however, the Author cannot guarantee its accuracy and validity and cannot be held liable for any errors or omissions. Changes are periodically made to this book. You must consult your doctor or get professional medical advice before using any of the suggested remedies, techniques, or information in this book.

Table Of Contents

Chapter 1: LinkedIn Basics

On a famous be aware, the evolution of social media has opened new possibilities for advertising and advertising and marketing and vending of business corporation to experts. In the equal vein, it has helped most business enterprise proprietors and professionals to understand how these structures work. At least, essential expertise is wanted. However, it must be said that not like Facebook, Twitter, and Instagram, LinkedIn has not been used optimally.

This is genuinely a few aspect to fear about in particular as it's far the satisfactory platform for B2B marketers to thrive. Interestingly, it's far the best platform suitable for B2B entrepreneurs. It is for its immoderate prospect that it modified into received via the use of way of Microsoft for $26billion.

After a careful have a check of the platform and the way with which inexperienced persons put it to use, one element is common

– maximum clients create profile which does no longer deliver them full-size pass again. This may be related to the seeming complexity of the platform in element or the sheer disinterest of the clients in spending time to create a professionally interesting profile.

Yet, regardless of the seeming complexity, it can't be denied that LinkedIn remains one of the critical digital property which virtually every person need to have. Yes, a should-have, in case you intend to take your career to a greater height.

So, in case you are not at the platform but or in case your LinkedIn account is dormant, now may be the time to get immoderate. Are you prepared to recognize more approximately this remarkable social network for business corporation and professionals? Let's get started out.

What is LinkedIn?

LinkedIn has about 610 million clients, and that's sincerely low for an internet community that's described because of the reality the principle platform for experts.

Please study that the variety maintains developing every day. In fact, experts have become a member of the platform at a charge of human beings constant with seconds. And these users are allotted throughout about hundred global locations of the arena. Among those customers are people in severa jobs, professions, arts, and industries. As you could see, it's a completely large platform wherein you can tap into multiple possibilities.

To a bigger extent, LinkedIn has prompted a revolution approximately how social media marketing and content material advertising and advertising operations can be finished. Presentation is top specially if you are a process seeker or looking to discover new fields, making try and beautify your visibility or your social network.

LinkedIn opens up a cute channel in an effort to are searching out employment, stay related with experts in the discipline, and recruit geared up abilities. Whatever place you are in, if you want to development on this digital age, you haven't any excuse no longer to be on LinkedIn.

How Does LinkedIn Enable Networking?

We can liken LinkedIn to a mixer, genuinely in spite of the fact that. It permits you to connect to people that you recognize or intend to recognize. In this magnificence are humans to your smartphone contact or mail listing. Irrespective of their numbers, LinkedIn allows you to connect to them.

But to set up a a fulfillment connection, you need to installation a extremely good profile. And that's in which maximum people get it wrong. Let's face it, LinkedIn isn't always as complex as we expect it's far. The one issue we've got did now not do is the want to test the manner it without a doubt works.

To construct an remarkable profile, ensure you're making a compelling and correct summary of your self, which encompass your profession – past, present, and destiny if need be. Please, in no manner forget about approximately to country important factors about yourself, your schooling, venture experience, awards, and publications. And don't forget about that no experience is unimportant.

Also, ensure that you add a easy image of your self. Build your profile above common, you might not be a expert however in your area but gather a famous profile.

Above all else, be energetic. If you're on LinkedIn but inactive, you want to be to your mark now. Your diploma of activeness has hundreds to do with how speedy you can grow to be a character to reckon with in your preferred organization.

How do you end up energetic, you would possibly want to ask? Post content fabric that are useful to those in your marketplace niche or industry. Comment and like posts of these you've got were given were given related to to your agency. Share what they are saying with others. Join a discussion board which can permit your need for increase and visibility. These are essential to-dos because of the reality doing them constantly boom your boom degree.

What is LinkedIn Used for?

To Grow Your Network

Network is important to any shape of growth you need to revel in to your state of affairs. Isn't that why conferences, seminars, and boards at the moment are attended thru specialists globally? And the fact is which you don't want to wait till you grow to be a professional in your preferred assignment earlier than you network.

LinkedIn gives all and sundry with interest a big possibility to grow and increase. You is probably an expert networker or a newbie, as long as you are prepared to take a risk, the ball is in your courtroom. It simplest prices you suitable net connection and a surfing cell phone, essentially.

Join or Create a Forum

Like we said earlier, the setting difference amongst Facebook and LinkedIn is that the latter permits you to hook up with specialists to your field. So, like what you are used to on Facebook, LinkedIn moreover offers you an possibility to sign up for a communicate board, enterprise, network that hobbies you. Besides, you can additionally create your non-public in case you trust on your personal voice.

However, you have to make sure that some thing organization you be part of, there can be mutual hobby. Don't be silent on any business enterprise, take part in some aspect they do and ensure which you make a contribution to discussions meaningfully.

To Create Opportunities

If you are searching out possibilities, LinkedIn is the proper location to be. This isn't to say other networks are not crucial. But if you are intentional approximately your growth in any trouble, LinkedIn is a platform that you should begin to take seriously. While you are trying to find possibilities, there are top managers and experts in industries who are at the platform to create possibilities. So, the possibilities that await you are so large. When you're constantly active, your connections can be willing to refer you for possibilities while it gained't be hard that allows you to moreover are attempting to find.

To Grow Business Ventures

LinkedIn offers business enterprise owners and entrepreneurs numerous options to develop and enlarge their corporations. If your targets are exceptional businesses, then LinkedIn is the right area to be. Let no man or woman tell you in any other case. On LinkedIn, you may execute your advertising and marketing and advertising and marketing and advertising strategies like content material cloth advertising and advertising and marketing. Not amazing that, you could purchase centered commercials at the equal time as using tools provided via the platform to music the quantity of views, diploma of engagement, and attain at the equal time.

Status Updates

Like it is been so far emphasised, consistency is fundamental on LinkedIn. You have to be lively and one of the assets you do to live lively is updating fame. If you want to build a elegant profile, you will need to be aware of posting informative and relevant content material fabric. It may be a short or extended well-composed article approximately property you are enthusiastic about. Don't neglect that hobby is prime and make certain you've got were given completed your homework well earlier than you put up something.

When it comes to staying lively through constant posting, some one of a kind issue you need to phrase is the need to respond at the same time as people react. Don't publish and be lengthy gone. Respond to remarks and questions. When your connections see which you well known their voice, they may continuously be willing to react to something you placed up.

If the case is in any other case, you may be fortunate to get 3likes on the same time as next you positioned up on LinkedIn.

Blog

Do you have got a flair for on foot a blog, LinkedIn lets in you to share what you write at the equal time as you moreover may additionally have get right of entry to to what others are strolling a blog approximately. This is one of the first-rate techniques to set up yourself as a perception chief in your preferred situation or any new problem of hobby you're focused on.

To Build a Platform

There isn't always any restrict to what you can do on LinkedIn as long as it is expert. So, right right right here is an opportunity to optimally use your ardour.

LinkedIn lets in you to construct a platform wherein you could skip nice message in the course of for your connections and fanatics. The gear are there that permits you to apply.

To Locate Your Tribe

There is constantly a tribe for every vicinity of hobby. This isn't always about the ethnic agency you belong to. The humans of the tribe being mentioned proper here are folks who share the equal price and interest with you.

Wouldn't or now not it is super to link up with them? Through the tribe, you get to recognize your community, extend your personal facts as you studies from each other. The possibilities are massive, the query is: which tribe do you need to be stated with?

Job Search

Don't be amazed via the masses of pastime opportunities available on LinkedIn. While a few are there to gather their private brand, masses more are there to search for gadget possibilities. That's why it modified into said from the start that you want to spend tremendous time on growing a profile this is general. And don't forget about that your profile consists of your CV, resume, task experience, educational information, credentials, and awards, among others.

However, don't neglect the want to be energetic and visible. People who have were given challenge possibilities on LinkedIn didn't get it on a platter of gold. You want to be lively and seen within the beginning. So, don't surely create a elegant profile and bypass.

When you are energetic for your internet page and in systems/tribes that you belong to, you have a first rate threat of being endorsed and endorsed for jobs thru any of your connections. One brilliant trouble is that at the same time as you're seen, the process opportunities that come your manner might not be publicized on LinkedIn. People are searching regardless of the entirety, so if there may be a gap in their enterprise, they recommend you in-residence.

For Following the Leaders

You want to pay attention from the leaders in industries, groups, and professions. They are human too who take time to percent their thoughts and nicely-researched truth via LinkedIn posts to persuade human beings like you who are inquisitive about profession boom. So, if becoming powerful on your concern of hobby is a high-quality deal to you, get on LinkedIn.

Profiles Search

You are looking for to stay related with leaders? Or centered on a particular organisation on your B2B/B2C advertising and marketing approach, LinkedIn gives you seek tools to try this. You can carry out a targeted are seeking out that allows you hook up with the proper the professionals and companies.

When you are seeking out through profiles, you're capable of see their educational history, art work revel in, awards and courses, similarly to provide issue of engagement.

Companies & Brands

There are businesses and types on LinkedIn. Not fine are you capable of find out them and be part of, you get to look their normal updates approximately their control, market studies, and vacant positions, among others.

Individuals

There are also individuals on LinkedIn who have grow to be personal brands. We can name them influencers or visionary leaders, proper? It's common to appearance the "Influencer" badge on their profiles. Well, you may also get there.

Through the same platform, people who've attained this recognition are allowed, frequently, with the aid of the use of LinkedIn to percent weblog posts, replace recognition, and movement pics. You can commonly connect to them for to beautify your career and employer.

Basic Features Available on LinkedIn

Some of the clean features available on LinkedIn are examined under:

● Home: As speedy you join up and log in to the platform, you're geared up to start making connections. Your newsfeed will then begin to show you the sports activities of your connections. Remember that the ones consists of humans, specialists, and the pages of agencies you're following.

● Profile: Once you have got were given taken it gradual to create elegant profile, this selection suggests your name, vicinity, image, what you're engaged in, your academic history, among others. As you development in your profession, this feature additionally lets in you to feature or eliminate records.

• Jobs: Ton of jobs are posted with the aid of way of using people, professionals, and organizations each day. This function allows you to look them. With your profile facts similarly to precise placing you've got initiated for your profile, LinkedIn moreover recommends jobs to you.

• My Network: With this selection, you will see all the connections you have got. To see different options that you can add for your touch, all you have to do is place the mouse over this option and the alternatives will pop-up.

• Search Bar: This is your are seeking engine that allows you notice huge consequences based on the sector you are centered on. For more particular search for jobs, corporations, and experts, there may be an Advanced alternative close to the hunt bar. This is a completely reliable function.

• Messages: This function permits you to begin a communique with the ones you're related with. This can be executed thru private messages. Pictures and files may be related through this.

● Notifications: Just like unique social media systems, LinkedIn notifies you whilst any of your connections sends you an invite to join a set, to test a put up, or recommends you for some issue. This moreover consists of invitation to connect through manner of a professional or approval of your connection request with a person.

The above are primary abilities that you are privy to whilst you signal-up for a LinkedIn account. There are extra superior abilities that you want as a professional, however you want to enhance to top elegance account in advance than you can access them.

Resourceful Features for Everybody and Business

UNLIKE the smooth skills that you may get proper of get entry to to as quick as you open your LinkedIn account, there are other property which can be used to professionally enhance the increase of absolutely everyone and organization.

- LinkedIn Learning: When you are on the right platform, it's now not hard to discover solutions to essential questions regarding something. That's the possibility which LinkedIn getting to know provide.

Exceedingly, this feature permits you to look for software software program, competencies, and applications which you are interested by. You truly can't recall what awaits you till you navigate via to the LinkedIn getting to know home net net page.

Almost the entirety you're looking for has been located underneath classes like developments, editor's alternatives, and have a look at interior half-hour. If you want to keep your mind and thoughts sharp in particular as it worries your employer, LinkedIn studying home net page is generally endorsed.

● Active Status: Don't permit your green dot be located attempting. Just like Facebook, LinkedIn gives you the same feature. At the net net page of your connections, you can constantly see the green dot beside the photo of parents which can be active.

The case is the equal when you have set your lively fame to be seen. To flip it on, see the steps under:

1.   Go to "Settings & Privacy" page under your photograph.

2.   On the privateness page, go with the flow downward till you find out "How others see your LinkedIn interest."

3.   Select "Manage lively recognition."

four.   And store the changes wherein applicable.

● Career Advice: taking into consideration a contemporary-day profession path, you could continuously get recommendation from specialists in that venture through LinkedIn. In the equal way, when you have want advice to offer, you may in the end be associated with a person within your area of information.

When you start to use your statistics and records to help others on LinkedIn, it wouldn't be prolonged in advance than you attraction to large invitation to connect. Ultimately, you can use it as a form of online advertising and marketing.

● LinkedIn Publishing: While this selection has existed for a long term, many people did now not key into it. Not way to its seeming problem then. However, it's been made less difficult through LinkedIn. This is an opportunity that permits you to position up proper content material and with a easy alternate to the publishing settings, all of us who is not even on LinkedIn can view and examine. What do you advantage from undertaking a considerable fashion of customers? Your profits encompass more organisation possibilities and connections, extended conversion fee for your business company, and superior credibility as a notion-leaders. It's that smooth.

● Advanced Search: Carrying out on-line searches might be daunting. This shouldn't be new if you want to shop on-line. But no longer anything to worry about right right here. LinkedIn offers you the opportunity to look professionally via its Advanced search. Just by means of the usage of which include filters, you control what indicates up the instant you carry out a are searching for query within the searching for bar.

Also, this selection allows you to be positioned without troubles through potential customers. Meanwhile, this simplest works bets in case your profile is complete. We will talk greater approximately this in subsequent additives.

Now, allow's recollect some of the advantages delivered to you with the aid of LinkedIn.

Benefits of LinkedIn to your Marketing Strategy

Whether you're managing a present day commercial enterprise organization or it's been existent for a long term, an extensive advertising and marketing method is important. Unfortunately, an crucial resources which marketers ignore while mapping their advertising and advertising and marketing method is LinkedIn.

One element they have got did now not recognize is that aside from doing all it takes to decorate their purchaser base and community, LinkedIn can be a part of them to professionals who can assist their business organization gather achievement.

But then, you need to be geared up to run your account with functionality and talent which are required for industrial company fulfillment.

Apart from that, in what distinct methods are you capable of gain from creating a LinkedIn account and being lively on line? See them underneath.

It Offers a Friendly Environment for Your Business to Thrive

From inception, LinkedIn turned into designed for professionals and businesses. Apart from that, its set of policies isn't as complicated while in evaluation to what obtains on one-of-a-type structures like Facebook and Instagram. This has been made feasible that permits you to ensure that your achieve as an person or employer spreads through your companies on-line with out jeopardizing the wanted diploma of social connections.

Everything that your agency needs to obtain success in the virtual place is on LinkedIn.

It Makes Discovering New Talent Easy

In a studies completed via LinkedIn, social media websites have encountered about 72% growth of their use as interest placement and recruitment structures.

Until now, profession systems changed into the places wherein new abilities may be found. The case is now pretty wonderful, thanks to the evolution of social media. Professional net sites like LinkedIn can now be used to find new capabilities for recruitment into new and modern-day organizations.

It Enables Personal and Professional Credibility

If you're seeking out personal and expert credibility, you must be on LinkedIn. Many humans and companies are but to take gain of the opportunities offered through this platform. Now which you apprehend, it's higher than being overdue. Join now!

How can you are taking gain of this unique opportunity?

•   Stand out via posting content fabric related to your market location of interest or greater instances each week. If you could do this every day, please do.

- Make positive your content is continuously compelling.

- Be consistent. Never pass over your ordinary instances.

- Use your organization profile to feature posts as a way to installation your self as an expert.

- Also put up on your profile that allows you to gather a robust connection with your fans.

- Don't overlook about to be steady.

You Can Push Traffic to Your Site

As lengthy as you're constantly posting to your profile and you've the eye and hobby of your followers and connections, you may begin to embody links so you can redirect them on your net website on line for brought data.

Remember which you want to had been posting constantly, gaining their take delivery of as actual with earlier than incorporating hyperlink building into your posting.

You Can Launch Products on LinkedIn

Professional social media systems like LinkedIn can be used to launch merchandise. Doing this can make plenty of impact than you could ever don't forget. It goals now not saying but it need to be stated that net web sites like LinkedIn has modified the face of methods product statistics can be shared. You don't even want to wait till the product receives to the market or vendors' stores. You can market first to exclusive groups and parents which might be your objectives.

It Aids Meaningful Professional Relationships

With LinkedIn, you may assemble enormous expert relationships. In addition, latest studies shows that it's miles a vital device to fortifying bodily connections.

It Boosts Brand's Visibility

A preferred profile and completely optimized commercial enterprise web page can help in slightly boosting your rating on Google's seek engine result pages (SERPs).

Please observe the use of barely because there are lots of ranking factors which may be located into interest thru the hunt engine earlier than any net net web page also can need to rank at the top.

Still, irrespective of how little a well-optimized LinkedIn account could suggest to Google score, you may agree with the difference it is able to make in your conversion charge.

In order to rank in the search consequences, word the following seo (are looking for engine marketing and marketing) strategies.

• Incorporate the proper/pinnacle beauty key phrases into your net web web page bio and outline.

• Use sturdy descriptive words for your net web web page bio and description.

- Don't depart every crucial sections clean.

- Incorporate hyperlink constructing techniques through linking your weblog and internet sites for your posts, profile, and descriptions.

You Can Use LinkedIn Posts to Get to all your Page's Followers

Unlike extraordinary structures, LinkedIn posts have the high-quality opportunity of getting to the feeds of all of your fanatics. This is because of the truth there may be no filtering of feed.

Whatever you publish or update in your LinkedIn agency's net web page, display up on their feeds mechanically. That is that if they're your enthusiasts. And it doesn't be counted in the event that they have had any form of engagement together with your put up currently or not.

So, while you update significant and useful posts, there's no worry approximately limit.

None of your target audience is restricted with the aid of the use of using set of rules.

Meanwhile, we are not implying that everybody you are aiming to purpose on LinkedIn might be online whilst you publish. To beat this, you need to be consistent with posting. That's just the way it's miles to triumphing together along with your content material cloth cloth advertising and marketing strive on LinkedIn.

A 2014 examine finished through the Content Marketing Institute and MarketingProfs discovered that 90 four% of B2B entrepreneurs use LinkedIn for circulating content material fabric fabric. Besides, the ones marketers ascribed the platform because the exceptional with regards to rating at the pinnacle net page of include looking for results.

As you may see, there is not some element preventing you from prevailing.

Chapter 2: How Can You Create LinkedIn Account?

To be part of the LinkedIn network, you need to set up an account. This is a small price to pay whilst in contrast with the possibilities you stand to benefit through connections and followership.

There is not every other way to doing it- you need an account on the way to grow a personal network.

In this financial smash, we are capable of be talking approximately simplified system that you want to comply with to create a Log-in and Business account on LinkedIn.

Guides to Setting up a LinkedIn Login

This is supposed to be a sensible technique. So, open your browser and go to LinkedIn.Com. Then, examine the stairs below to create your log-in data.

Step 1

Once you've got were given were given been directed to the web net web page of LinkedIn, navigate to the Join Now Button at the right factor of the internet net web page. Click on it and also you wait at the same time as you're directed to a page wherein you may be required to deliver fundamental facts in the containers furnished.

The necessities in the order of appearance are:

- First call

- Last call

- Email deal with

- A sturdy password with now not lots much less than six characters

How do you offer you with sturdy password?

Coming up with a sturdy password -100/one hundred, isn't always a complex. Just apprehend a way to mix uppercase, lowercase, quantity, and a few special person.

Step 2

Revealing statistics that hassle your area and employment reputation are the actions you want to absorb this step. The options available so that it will select from are:

- Employed

- Looking for Work

- Business Owner

- Working Independently

- A student

You need to know that the selection you pick out out out have to impact special fields that you could be required to fill. For example, in case you picked Employed as your option, the alternative fields that would pop-up include enterprise, u . S . A . Zip, code of your location, and venture name further to description.

On the other hand, if you picked A pupil as your preference, you may be required to offer the choice of the employer you attend, your area of hobby, the zip code of your vicinity, and u . S ..

Please examine that the zip code of your area is always a non-public information. So, regardless of the fact that the device indicates your place, it keeps your zip code as personal.

As you may see, the entire technique is simple. Meanwhile, there can be an possibility to head for LinkedIn Premium account. Here, you'll be asked to offer your street cope with further to the ones asked above.

Please, bypass over the information you provided another time for the sake of accuracy. And to prevent issues inside the future. Remember, LinkedIn is basically a platform for specialists and companies.

Once you get to the end of filling required statistics based on the choice you chose under this step, you may keep to click on Continue.

Step three

Under this step, you are required to connect your email so that you can import contacts out of your cellular telephone e-book. While the two steps above are compulsory, this step is at your very very own discretion. But then, in advance than you select the element you need to stand, consider what we said about constructing a expert and large profile?

Why need to you are taking this feature? It allows you increase your community effects. So, at the same time as you join, you will be capable of go through your address e-book to connect to or invite any e-mail that is associated with a LinkedIn profile.

Some of the emails allowed for LinkedIn are Gmail, Yahoo mail, Gmail, Hotmail and others which didn't pop-up within the lists furnished with the aid of way of manner of the machine.

Please take a look at that whatever possibility you select out, you could't get admission to your address ebook except you log in on your email account.

Also, be conscious that now not every e mail might match that of each person you observed may be on LinkedIn. This is because of the reality a few customers created their LinkedIn account with a particular e mail deal with.

Don't overlook that this step is optionally to be had, so that you can pass it if you so desire.

After you want to have preferred or skipped the e-mail deal with import desire, a affirmation display could seem telling you to verify your e-mail cope with on your e-mail area.

The confirmation mail can also supply right away or it'd take a few minutes. Whichever way, you want to take the time to affirm the message, enter your log-in information to get proper of entry for your LinkedIn profile. Once you're on your profile, start to connect to specialists.

Can we now retain to how you may create a corporation net web page or account?

How Do You Create A LinkedIn Company Account?

Having a LinkedIn agency account is vital to a company's advertising and marketing and advertising method. Refer to monetary spoil one in which we noted the blessings of a LinkedIn account to groups. You can't sincerely neglect them.

But in advance than you rush into logging immediately to the net web page to test to your industrial agency, make sure you have got were given got the proper to perform the LinkedIn web internet page creation. And additionally, get your emblem prepared. The duration of the brand that's in reality helpful is 300 x 300pixel and make sure it's a rectangular emblem.

Before you go over the steps involved under, you have to be reminded that having a

LinkedIn profile is a demand for growing a business enterprise.

Step 1

Creating LinkedIn organization business enterprise web page is simple and easy so long as you look inside the proper path.

To create an internet page, you need to navigate to the top proper corner of the internet web page wherein you can find out a tab labelled "Work".

Once you click on on, a listing will drop down with the intention to pick "Create a Company Page". This is at the lowest. Find the (+) sign, then click on on on on it.

Whether you're a Premium member or no longer, having a preferred non-public account is vital to putting in vicinity a web web page to your enterprise employer. Premium member or no longer, a private account is crucial to putting in a company page. However, if you definitely ought to create a state-of-the-art account for this reason, you will must look in advance to some weeks so that you can create a organisation internet internet web page.

Step 2

At this stage, you'll be required to supply all crucial records to your business organization net page. The first piece of data which you might deliver is the call of the corporation.

Pay cautious hobby to the identify case, ensure you enter the equal way you need LinkedIn to show your call.

In the second one container, you may be required to characteristic the organization URL. This isn't always complicated in any respect. The call of your industrial business enterprise need to were added robotically to the second one field with a sprint in the various texts that make the company name. It's ok if you need take out the dashes to make it straightforward and functionally related together collectively with your brand. Or you could simply pick a URL that is the much like what obtains on social web web sites like Facebook. Take a organization known as Building Nations Initiative for example, the URL will robotically seem as linkedin.Com/organization/constructing-countries-initiative.

And on your non-public, you can edit it to reappear as linkedin.Com/enterprise/buildingnationsinitiative.

After doing that, you want to continue to offer a technique of verification to reveal that you have the proper proper to attain this.

Also to be had is the option to create a University web net page. The talents to be had encompass a phase for alumni. You must touch LinkedIn in case you plan to set up this form of internet page.

Step three

Here, you need to take it slow to work on placing the outlook of the web internet page to align with the organisation. What is being stated is the branding your page. And you could't have sufficient money to neglect this.

To start with, you ought to set up the internet web page's cowl picture. Why is that this vital? The display of cowl pix aren't normally the same relying on whether or now not or now not you logged in on a pc or cellular browser. Now, you need to skip for length 1536 x 768 – this is the right length. And don't neglect approximately to layout a cover photograph that grabs everything of what your industrial company represents.

And a brief tip for the sensible: Resist the temptation to apply a cowl that has textual content or phrase.

Once you're accomplished with placing the quilt photograph, importing your commercial corporation brand is the subsequent. Remember we advocated that you get the emblem ready in advance than you even begin the internet page advent.

It isn't recommended that you use a personal profile, just like the image of your company's CEO, at the identical time as you prepare the brand. After all, you're managing specialists and groups on a professional platform.

Step four

Next, you have to offer LinkedIn with an in depth description of your organization and what it does. Don't forget about that some aspect you say proper here is going to be the primary issue of touch which any prospective consumer on that platform might likely have. So, don't neglect about the want to install your brilliant.

Of direction, you must have among 1500 – 2000 phrases description for this. But on occasion, that's no longer enough. Even if it's most effective a one thousand terms description, ensure it's applicable and compelling. Don't overlook approximately to apply the right SEO key terms too. More regularly, it's about the in-intensity first-rate description and not the period.

To make developing your description less difficult, define the objectives which your business employer desires to advantage through the web page. Map out your goal marketplace from the group of specialists and groups on LinkedIn, understand the perfect selling detail of your organisation, word the blessings your business enterprise; and more importantly, claim how the ones blessings enhance the lives of your goal.

Creating relevant and amazing description calls for mindset. And you don't need to rush the steps. Relax. And take some time to do this.

And don't sincerely write and publish. Do a self-edit, and hire a proofreader to go through it in case your business enterprise does now not have one.

After that, select the areas of particular hobby of your organisation. Pick as a whole lot as you may to your organization — there are approximately 20 unique areas of interest. But be right. Make nice that anything location of robust thing you pick out, your business enterprise actually has it. The social vicinity is full of fake claims already, don't increase the variety.

Step 5

Under this step, all you want to do is consist of critical facts which may be the kind and period of your organisation, the one year it changed into primarily based completely, website cope with, business enterprise/area, and region.

If your enterprise has locations allotted throughout a area or territory, you want to pick one important workplace – the head workplace.

Step 6

This step gives you the opportunity to function corporations on your enterprise agency internet page. The pages you can upload is probably the one you very own or the ones you're effective would possibly make a contribution definitely to the growth of your intention and ultimately, your web page.

Step 7

These are alternatives you could cross once more to attend to after publishing your internet web page. This step lets in you to encompass tagline, name to moves (CTAs), amongst others.

For your CTAs, you could consist of the any of these – observe more, touch/name us now, go to our internet net web page, take a look at in proper proper right here, join up, we are able to chat, amongst others.

You should make the most of the selection to motion feature via manner of the usage of inputting a URL that could ease the approach of directing users to a conversion funnel to your internet site.

Step 8: Content Creation

You don't need to be recommended that on your industrial employer to thrive, you have to include content material fabric marketing. Meanwhile, don't get all of it incorrect. Content goes past text layout. It encompasses photographs, quick movies, infographics, and others.

You ought to be aware that the amount of your business enterprise's boom has masses to do together with your degree of consistency with uploading content fabric. The boom of the enterprise internet page is based totally upon on the frequency of your content advertising and advertising.

To ensure regular content material material marketing and advertising, you can use software for scheduling your activities.

LinkedIn Premium Account

This is a paid plan which you can pick in case you are prepared to upgrade your loose version LinkedIn account. And this comes with large abilties. So, you can count on that it is probably actually nicely really worth the rate and try. Should making a decision to improve, you get to experience a month-loose trial.

Once the loose-trial expires, you begin to pay for subscription. The charge plan to be had are month-to-month and yearly. You should the handiest you agree with you studied you're great with.

Some of the talents available under this bundle are:

- Unrestricted open/direct messages.

- Access to top elegance content fabric.

- Premium search filters.

- Great are seeking out capability.

- Open club hyperlink.

- Opportunity to view your profile traffic.

- Response to questions in a business corporation day.

- LinkedIn badge.

- Unique and superior communications device, and others.

Now, based truly on your challenge of hobby, there are 4 debts that you could pick pick out from to your decorate. They are:

- Recruiter Lite

- Job Seeker

- Business Plus

- Sales Navigator

Recruiter Lite:

This top rate decorate draws a monthly rate. And it is mainly for groups who are in are looking for of new abilities for recruitment.

The individual interface design of Recruiter Lite package deal turn out to be designed with an cause – simplification of staffing manner.

The functions are slot management, targeted seek, InMail management, profile manage, reporting and analytics, and other collaborative gear.

Also, LinkedIn Recruiter Lite gives unrestricted get right of entry to to 30 InMail messages each month for each member of the team. What's extra? The InMail characteristic we must every member have interaction right now with specialists.

With this package deal deal, there can be unrestricted get right of access to to limitless profiles with advocated ones.

There are many more. And you could guess that LinkedIn acquired't forestall at the ones. The adventure in the direction of simplifying recruitment gadget has honestly began.

Job Seeker:

Are you a activity seeker? Do you apprehend absolutely everyone attempting to find interest opportunities? This bundle deal deal is for project seekers. While the prerequisite for use won't be the identical, operating it demands a month-to-month rate that allows you to apply certain abilities.

Some of the features are opportunity to expose your badge indicating that you are a activity seeker on your profile. Also, you have got the possibility to get right of access to people who considered your profile in 90 days. This is that this form of features which distinguishes a loose account from a top class. And have to you locate recruiters that hobby you, you have got were given the threat to message them proper now. The InMail function provides you 5 for each month and this comes with a confident credit rating rating skip back if no InMail reaction is available in seven days.

Business Plus:

It's not sufficient to be a professional. Life will become much less difficult at the same time as you are able to hook up with like-minds. To make this feasible, Business Plus package deal brings this terrific way to every person. With a month-to-month fee, you get delivered to twenty-five profiles, about 1/3 degree suggestions, and you can carry out extra are searching for for your self to help you decorate your network.

In addition, you get 15 InMails month-to-month along 7days reaction assure. Plus, you have got had been given as a wonderful deal as 30 e mail credits – unused ones will roll over into a few distinctive month.

What's extra? This enhance allows you to assess your overall performance collectively together together with your connections. This is possible due to the fact you get to look a month-to-month have a look at of your common performance.

Sales Navigator:

This enhance is an integration with the technology from Point Drive that lets in you to enhance your income purpose. With insights derived from the huge database that's to be had, this offers you an unrestricted risk to connect with possibilities that want your services.

This is generally recommended for the earnings representative of any business enterprise. With this tool, you get to assess and display the conversations of your goals while fundamental them carefully in your platform offline after which proper right right into a purchase channel.

LinkedIn furthermore makes use of your records to suggest leads on your business employer using this tool. Again, this enhance lets in you to get updates concerning high-rating selection makers walking with contacts for your listing. You shouldn't take this as a proper in case you care about ascertaining the type of clients you're speakme with. Or don't you need to be abreast of actions like content cloth shares, company and cutting-edge touch updates of the contacts on your listing?

Based at the analysis above, you shouldn't overlook that some component top price company you select out need to align together along with your want as an individual, expert, or company. It is commonly encouraged that you take some time to capture the way the premium capabilities function, that's why LinkedIn gives 1 MONTH FREE TRIAL.

How To Make Payment For Premium Account

Before you can make price, you'll be required to provide your LinkedIn password for verification. After this, you need to select out a rate opportunity of your choice. You have an choice amongst PayPal account and Credit Card. The opportunity you choose will determine the information you'll be required to post next.

A charge receipt can be sent in your electronic mail address along a printable one on your show display. If you need to shut the on-show receipt, you want to click on at the button which reads "I'm accomplished".

Following that, you will be directed to click at the "Start your free trial button". This is made available at the manner to assist you to get to understand how the plan you need to have decided on works.

This method that you can cancel if you grow to be now not liking your preference. In order not to get billed, make certain you cancel the plan earlier than the simplest month loose trial expires.

Chapter 3: How to Create a LinkedIn Profile That Sells

As said earlier, your LinkedIn profile is the primary risk you need to create an enduring have an effect on on any prospect who comes throughout your profile. Don't take the need to have a popular profile as a right. In reality, as a marketer, it's not your after-notion in any respect. Put in all the attempt you have got at your disposal into growing one. You don't want to hurry over doing this. This is in spite of everything, the primary hazard you've got got to say some thing unique and impacting approximately your logo.

Don't virtually say, display your possibilities through the carefully determined on phrases on your web web page which you understand what they may be going via and that you have the desired solution. So, some thing you have got to mention in your profile need to be unique enough to guide the opportunity to buy your products or services.

To promote and achieve fulfillment as a commercial enterprise, you need to construct an amazing profile in your LinkedIn account. You have the brilliant platform to build a strong network, it's yours to take.

Thus, this financial disaster will take you through how you could optimize your LinkedIn account and profile to do the following:

•   Have a strong community in your business enterprise or logo.

•   To advantage accept as true with that outcomes in conversion.

•   And in the end make earnings.

Vital Characteristics of a LinkedIn profile

A LinkedIn profile desires to have the subsequent traits if it need to obtain its intention as a possible earnings channel. These developments are considered underneath:

- A smooth show photo –headshot with a brilliant background, on your profile. And make sure it's a state-of-the-art one. Have a smile to your face too, you are trying to draw, undergo in thoughts?

- A historical past banner that during fact represents your emblem or in which you parent.

- A headline that isn't best compelling however furthermore of terrific. Your headline want to summarize the carrier you provide in easy and clean phrases.

- Additional media like video, audio, infographics, graphs, and so forth that accessory how you want to help your potentialities.

- Lastly, you need to create a profile precis that extends the narrative of the way you will be of help for your people searching for products/services.

Does A Good Profile Influence Sales?

There isn't always any magic to boosting sales, all you could find is advertising and advertising and marketing techniques that you may embody to get there. And even as being on LinkedIn is this type of strategies, having a awesome profile in your account is an delivered benefit.

In fact, with the beneficial useful resource of now, you need to have determined that there are various skills that LinkedIn allows you to take advantage of in case your enterprise and brand need to stay on in this age of social media evolution.

The way through which you can appeal to prospects are large, and having an brilliant profile is the primary issue of contact. So, positive, a GOOD profile affects earnings.

Note the emphasis on accurate. This is extra approximately the way you create your profile using the proper content material with a cue about how your goals make informed purchasing for choice and the form of key terms they enter within the are trying to find engine as they progress from the first step at the profits funnel to the remaining.

With your profile, you may each set up yourself as a person they want to go through to fulfill their wishes or they're able to pass beforehand to are searching out for assist someplace else.

In the chapters to conform with, we're capable of undergo how the form of so impacts the selection to start a verbal exchange with you or not. You clearly want to do that right with carefulness. Just so that you apprehend. We will communicate about this sizable later.

So, what do you do to have the proper profile that brings you beneficial connections and lovers? Pay interest to the following. Are you organized?

Build Your Profile Through The Eyes of the Buyers

You don't without a doubt jump into growing a profile due to the fact LinkedIn requires you to create a profile. As a marketer, you even need to be more intentional right right here. Don't sincerely communicate approximately your profession achievements, in which is the area of your targets? The query your purpose are going to be asking is beyond what your qualifications are. The query is: What are you presenting us attributable to your career achievements?

To win, you need to shift the narrative in your profile. Be extra consumer-focused. What you have to flaunt is your capability to offer the answers that they want. They want a better lifestyles, they want to develop and enhance their requirements; that's why they're for your profile within the first area.

If your content cloth fails to show them the ones, ensure that they'll drift on.

Okay, its extremely good to talk approximately your achievements, but don't allow that be the closing. Show, don't simply tell, the manner you desire to add simply to their lives, companies, among others. Your

LinkedIn profile should show your potential clients the way you want to help them. How revolutionary are you about casting off their disturbing situations? And to them, your answer is all that topics.

Incorporate a Stunning Headshot Photo

As noted in advance, having the right profile picture is a part of the deal. And it must be a professional shot. This is not any such photographs you are taking at the side of your cellphone. Plus, it want to be modern. We are emphasizing present day as it ought to align with what you genuinely look like want to any of your connection determine to have a physical meeting with you.

We advocate within the direction of using a logo as your profile photograph due to the fact this is about you as a brand in vicinity of a business enterprise. Besides, doing so is in opposition to LinkedIn's purchaser's agreement.

Meanwhile, you haven't any excuse for leaving your profile photograph field empty. You are on a social media platform for professionals, maximum of them can be interested in seeing the image of who they are dealing with. Besides, in case you want to enjoy a forty% risk of having quick responses to your InMail, and having more profile views, you have to have a expert profile picture.

Note the following expert profile picture tips for LinkedIn and each different:

• Smile warmly with minimal publicity of your tooth.

• Keep your eyes at the virtual digicam.

• The photograph should awesome circulate out of your head to shoulders.

• Go with head-waist frame if need be.

• Don't use sun sun sun shades.

• Use a white historical past, avoid colored garb.

And don't forget about about to use historic past banner. It allows you draw hobby on your brand early sufficient. If you've got a corporation you determine with, encompass the colors and emblem of the emblem into your header to make it complete.

Create a Great Headline

Like in records reporting, the headline is vital to attracting visitors on your profile. So, right right here, the way you headline your profile topics. Not handiest want to it's catchy, clean, and wealthy, it have to be compelling. While this seems like what every body could create without pressure, irrespective of everything, it's genuinely no longer extra than 100 and twenty characters or lower; you want to do it carefully.

Among one among a type subjects, it need to inspire them to need to apprehend extra approximately you, the issuer you provide, and how you can solve their issues.

By now, you have to understand that your headline is not a few detail you create in a hurry as well. Take it slow, pick out the proper key phrases to use based totally totally in your marketplace place of interest, and encompass the shape of terms that your goals can discover with even though wearing out a searching for.

In order to win with the right headline, you need to use the proper key phrases, encompass the call of your agency, and encompass how you may be of help in your potentialities.

Are you questioning how you are purported to do the ones internal a a hundred and twenty characters restriction? It's feasible, don't you observed?

What about announcing, as an instance:

An Account Integrator that Helps Bank Users in America to Analyze Transactions and Eliminate Wasteful Subscriptions/Emma Inc.

What has the headline above carried out?

- It stated who the dreams are.

- It additionally said what the company does.

- It identified the geographical region.

- It identified the hassle. And thinking about the truth that goals want answers to bank overdraft fees and one of a kind wasteful hidden fees, they might actually involved to look in addition proper right into a profile with that form of headline.

Can you do extra than that during a hundred and twenty characters? Yes.

Make Your Profile Summary Compelling

Yes, you want to apply this 2000 characters foreign exchange you have to make a compelling profile precis. In facts, permit your objectives comprehend your engagement, the industrial business enterprise business enterprise you decide for, after which, who you're. Don't forget to make this appear to be about your goal market – the benefits you convey to them, if you need to stress prolonged conversion fee.

seo is surprisingly vital proper right here. Use the proper key terms to pressure domestic the goals of your potentialities. Show them, thru your profile precis that you are an important useful resource to sending away their problems. That manner you need to be compelling. Using the right key terms help your profile summary to rank pinnacle in are looking for outcomes each time a prospect launches a are attempting to find query.

Your Use of English is a Criteria

In all you do, don't overlook approximately which you are on a social media platform for specialists who pay excessive interest to information. While you're there to draw potentialities, you shouldn't take your use of English as a right. What we strive to mention is that you want to understand the recommendations of grammar. This consists of tenses, punctuations, spellings, and others.

You in no way can inform how a single mistakes ought to show a big prospect off. You never can! So, it's exceptional now not to be careless. Put the proper time into checking and re-checking each of your content. Hire a expert content material cloth editor even even as you have to have done your self-enhancing.

No do not forget how outstanding the content material seems to you, don't be in a rush to replace it. Don't be too lazy to head over any content material cloth material again and again once more. If you want to make an tremendous have an effect on to your profile, you can't be too careless with facts.

Everything subjects, don't forget about this.

Meanwhile, you should write with reason. What do you want them to look through your profile summary? If they're able to't see that you can constitute yourself in a tremendous moderate, how do you anticipate them to trust you with representing them nicely?

How you write and use language –client focused, will each cause them to live or pass to a few other profile. Ultimately, the reason is to steer them enough to guide them to take movement. If the message you would like to skip in the course of is heavy with grammatical errors, you don't assume that they might be willing to take moves. Do you?

Include Media

To make your profile whole, along side media is the manner to move. Besides, this will similarly mold your credibility and help you benefit don't forget. With the URL, you could add video, presentation, and visuals related to your commercial corporation.

This is part of you showing them how you can resolve their issues. The media you upload might be about your previous responsibilities for a purchaser. And wherein a image speaks louder than a thousand terms, you could believe how masses extra a video must do?

You can continuously add media for your profile precis or on the Experience segment.

Optimize the Experience Section

Here is your chance to inform your opportunities about yourself and what you are engage in. With 2000 characters freedom to express, make certain you highlight your attributes, offerings, and USPs.

Below is a list of the way you want to govern your Experience section:

• What you do similarly to who you're.

• Previous interest research and the jobs you completed in consumer satisfaction.

• Include hyperlink to media that's related to what you do/who you are.

You need to understand there are quite a number of LinkedIn account pushing for the equal component, so do it nicely. To be taken more professionally, you have to hyperlink the LinkedIn internet page of your enterprise. With this, the brand of your employer is probably on show mode and this goes an extended way to provide you a extra strategic positioning.

Understand Your Company's Policies

Never take any on line motion that is going closer to the in-house coverage of your business enterprise. So, earlier than you add any commercial enterprise enterprise organisation under your contemporary project description, make sure it's ok to obtain this.

Check and re-check any declare you are making about any organization or feature. It's important to assemble a criticism-free LinkedIn profile if you want to gain the attraction of trying to find what you offer.

Leave no Field Untouched

For a professional social media internet site on line like LinkedIn, not anything can take the location of getting a totally-finished profile. Ensure you go away no subject untouched – that's the first rate recommendation all people can provide you with. Why is this essential? Prospective customers are greater eager to pay attention to a marketer whose profile is entire than the only who isn't. Do you understand that?

So, take a while to talk about your educational data; you have got 2000 characters to do this. Talk approximately how the moments spent in faculty original you.

Add your abilties, and don't neglect approximately the need to constantly replace them. There is typically room for increase, isn't it? While you could encompass as many talents as you need, ensure to stick to the relevant to you.

What's extra? More similar to the likes that you get on Facebook from pals and speak to to your sports, you can provide your endorsements to human beings you recognize after highlighting your talents. Meanwhile, you could simplest do that whilst you need to have grew to emerge as on the suggest function to your setting.

Recommendation is a few other area to your profile creation that brings you a whole lot of powerful effects. First, be willing to put in writing coronary coronary heart-felt recommendation for the ones you've got got met and labored with on your profession path. It's even viable that you are in spite of the truth that working with them. At the same time, don't hesitate to attempting to find the advice of these who've worked with you too. Just make sure their tips align with competencies you have were given indicated to your profile.

• Why need to you deliver and are looking for hints?

Search engines are possibly to index your advice segment even as people carry out are looking for queries approximately what you do. If the right key terms have been used on this section, this is an brought benefit that permits you appear pinnacle in seek outcomes pages.

Every successful marketer on LinkedIn is aware this to be a important tool which could help bring the kind of leads with a promising price of conversion.

Standard Profile Is Important to the Success of Your Sales

Once once more, as a marketer, having a sizeable profile on LinkedIn is huge on your achievement. If you've got have been given been failing at selling on LinkedIn, it's time to head and re-look at your profile. Don't get incorrect even though. We are not pronouncing that's the answer, it's just the superb location to start at if you need to trade the narrative.

Most times, the success you revel in as a marketer who gets the eye of the marketplace begins offevolved at the side of your profile.

Chapter 4: Determining Your Ideal Customers

Having established the suggestions for growing a customer-focused profile, we are capable of guess which you already recognize how this is going an extended way to decorate your conversion fee.

So, it's time to speak approximately the way to determine the satisfactory clients in your commercial enterprise business employer. We recognize that for maximum entrepreneurs, the hassle isn't always generally approximately growing a consumer-targeted profile, but figuring out who a notable client is.

Please, despite the fact that we referred to connecting with the ones you apprehend through using a function that allows you to hyperlink your touch list in your LinkedIn account, you must apprehend that there will continuously be an exception.

Here is the caution: When it entails identifying the proper customer for your business employer, your families and pals don't usually have an area. In truth, they'll be generally the simplest who have little or no interest internal the goods or offerings you offer.

You need to prevent making assumption as a marketer. Don't positioned your advertising hopes in the identical basket together together with your families and pals in order no longer to be disappointed. So, how do you ascertain the right clients to your products and services?

This chapter gives unique techniques that can help you pick out your exceptional customers. Are you prepared?

Create A Profile of Your Ideal Client

There isn't any one of a kind manner to it than first developing a profile that you can lure a high-quality patron. And at the equal time as we've talked, in the previous financial ruin approximately the way to create a standard profile, you continue to want to need to do a self-evaluation the usage of the questions set beneath. The solutions you're able to supply to those questions will help you decide your awesome patron.

• What class of clients usually have the hassle my product or service solves?

• What sort of person could be geared up to pay for my products and services at the set price?

You want to discover the answers to those questions due to the reality even as you could have the products or services that solves the troubles of each person, now not all people may be inquisitive about looking for. Besides, no longer all and sundry may be geared up and able to pay the charge you have set on your services or products. With the answers to the questions above already decided, you need to now examine the subsequent:

• In what area or u.S. Do my first-class clients live? Consider their metropolis and time-zone.

•   What age-bracket do my splendid customers belong?

•   Would you as an opportunity intention humans, organizations, or companies?

•   And in the end, what's the gender of my brilliant clients?

Have it in the again of your mind that you could't have all people in the marketplace to your self. Almost anybody is already taking, all you want to do is take a element. That's why it's crucial to choose out your best customers.

So, what's subsequent?

Add them together

At this factor, you want to add your products or services provided with the profile that's focused on your ideal patron. Once again, include ok facts.

Let's assume which you have determined out that the paintings time inside the metropolis of your quality clients is 12.00pm –

three.00am EST, you may set your line like this:

Ryan is a brand expert in xxxxx and may best provide services to clients from 12.00pm – 3.00am EST.

Please, there is no element in speeding everywhere. There isn't any plan to shut down LinkedIn, neither are your goals going everywhere. Whether they located you first in any other case you probable did, the roads that leads there is a favored profile that's consumer-centered.

Identify Your Collaborators – Companies or Individuals

After coming across your tremendous customers and the usage of them as guide to create your profile, the subsequent element is to look for the humans or companies you would like to collaborate with. Use the search tool on Google to discover potential collaborators, then you could hook up with those appropriate for your commercial enterprise on LinkedIn.

How Do You Establish Connection?

Once all over again, not business agency an first rate consumer as some distance as B2B advertising is worried. So, you want to first understand the thing of connection you have in respect to hobby. Is it a number one, second, or zero.33 diploma connection? Do you have got got any personal relationship?

If there can be a private dating, you must undergo in thoughts analyzing them thru LinkedIn or a name. Don't honestly ask approximately own family and vintage buddies and stop it there. This need to be a way to soliciting for for an advent to the pinnacle preference maker in his/her business enterprise, so do it nicely just like the professional you are.

If there may be no individual you've got got a close to tremendous to introduce you to the individual or enterprise business enterprise, you may take a look at thru the LinkedIn fanatics of the employer. Be assured that there may be or extra personnel of the corporation moreover following the corporation's updates. Evaluate them, pick out out out a possible worker which could lead you to the employer and connect with him or her.

Identify Ideal Customers Using Area(s) of Shared Interest

In as a first rate deal as we are particular people, we usually have human beings with whom we share interest. And as a marketer, that is truly absolutely really worth tapping into. Isn't this the purpose seasoned salespersons have continuously counseled that we market only what we consider in? Verily, whilst you find out a aim who stocks your notion, it will become much less hard to convert them.

Meanwhile, it doesn't need to be completely or proper now an interest within the products or services you promote. The common floor may be going for walks in an corporation just like yours or a business enterprise organisation that requires your products or services.

It will also be the grad university which you each attended or a mutual buddy or enterprise membership on a few digital or bodily location.

No depend how small the shared hobby it, discover a way around it.

Path to Successfully Marketing to Your Ideal Clients

The adventure has just commenced after figuring out your extraordinary consumer and connecting with them on LinkedIn.

Don't virtually throw what you promote of their face, it's a direction you want to string with care. So, what are the advertising and marketing and advertising and marketing strategies you can tackle LinkedIn?

- Post articles continually.

•	Add innovative pictures, movement photos, webinars, and so on.

•	Comment, like, and percentage what they do as properly.

•	Don't forget approximately to answer to their feedback on yours.

•	Make certain anything you do is relevant on your market place of hobby and beneficial to them.

When you do the above with strength of will and consistency, it wouldn't be lengthy to benefit their trust and loyalty. Eventually, they may be inquisitive about what you're advertising and marketing whilst the time comes.

How Do You Find Your Niche on LinkedIn?

While LinkedIn could have been created with specialists in mind, it doesn't imply it's strictly for specialists. Based in this incorrect perception, some of marketers do pass over out on many opportunities that LinkedIn offers.

In fact, human beings and plenty of extra are however to enroll in this first-rate platform for the equal cause. And we can't blame them. LinkedIn focuses greater on B2B networking.

But, similarly, it is also a creative platform for people in numerous market region of hobby. And it's now not complex to discover your manner around networking find it impossible to resist's assumed with the useful resource of those who have did not be part of up.

Now, allow's speak how you may select out out your location of hobby and hints for establishing connections with those in it.

How to Identify Your Niche On LinkedIn

Follow Thought-leaders in Your Industry

From the start, LinkedIn launched an RSS reader called LinkedIn Today. The aim of this modified into to pile content material cloth at some stage in the complete users on the platform and simplest to percentage the handiest relevant on your marketplace vicinity of hobby with you.

Later, in 2013, LinkedIn Pulse -a feed app became released. So, you have were given an possibility to customise your newsfeed with the aid of yourself. To try this, you may use the following metrics:

- Channels

- ●Authors

- Influencers

It's viable that you'll locate your market place of interest in all the instructions above. However, the incredible location to appearance is with the influencers. This is because even as you place it to influencers for your region of interest, it's miles feasible to get get admission to to infinite subjects so long as they're labelled under your area of hobby.

What's extra? You will discover like-minds who are also doing the equal hassle – identifying with influencers on your marketplace vicinity of hobby, to network with and sooner or later marketplace to.

Use Targeted Keywords to Discover Specific Niche-Relevant Groups

You can hook up with members of your market location of hobby thru companies, tribes, and corporations. They are clean to discover – input applicable key phrases into the search bar supplied through LinkedIn. When the results pop-up, you still the choice to test thru. Once you determined the only that meets your place of interest, supply club request right away.

Once again, don't attempt to throw what you promote in their face as quickly as you be part of in case you are a marketer. And don't be in a haste to begin posting content fabric. Learn. Understand how the in-residence policy works. But that's no longer a cause to be inactive. While ready and learning, do the following:

- Comment.

- Ask question.

- Seek clarifications wherein you don't recognize what the writer or admin is attempting to say.

And do it all professionally. It's less tough to like and pass on that's why it's now not at the bullet list above. You want to do more than like, observation.

Try Direct Connections

It's ok in case you don't want to go through the steps above. You can take the direct route thru sending direct connection request to the goals in your market vicinity of hobby. Remember we referred to this in advance?

On the opportunity hand, you could use the people you could recognize characteristic. This is a aid made to be had with the resource of LinkedIn and that they cowl people who share a connection via particular related contacts or belong to a set with you. At least, you don't want to provide an reason for to this humans why you're sending a connection request.

Based on what we've got were given blanketed to this point, you'll accept as actual with us that LinkedIn is a definitely pleasant platform for connecting together with your best customers. It offers feasible win-win situation if tremendous you will make the effort to have a look at what your high-quality client is probably to input within the are searching for engine, the sort of content material fabric cloth your pleasant patron is probably greater interested by, the shape of aspiration that he or she fancies, amongst others.

It's a deliver-take situation as properly. When you do it nicely, you're in your way to growing connections that cause conversion in the long run.

Chapter 5: Best LinkedIn practices

LinkedIn is a big social media internet website for experts and people with profession mindset. Unlike Facebook, Instagram, and awesome social media structures that connect you to all form of humans, LinkedIn uses a direction.

How? This is an algorithmically driven manner in which, primarily based totally without a doubt on your profile, you are associated with folks who proportion the identical mindset with you.

What's the implication of this? It way you need to observe the splendid practices recommended thru the platform as a way to be strategically positioned. Whatever is your purpose – to build a network of leads on your industrial organization, content material material cloth advertising and marketing, interest seeking out, amongst others, it's crucial which you adhere to bet practices on LinkedIn.

LinkedIn can not be scorned if you or your business enterprise is inquisitive about constructing a professional community. And to thrive on LinkedIn, adhering to excellent practices is a need to. As a quit end result, this economic disaster talks about a number of the excellent practices you need to include alongside the errors that want to be avoided.

Are LinkedIn Best Practices Necessary?

According to About LinkedIn, 2019, there are approximately three million organization pages on LinkedIn. Thus, there can be no incorrect, becoming a member of this social medium is one of the superb subjects that could arise to any commercial enterprise corporation. Yes, if you want your commercial employer to develop and increase.

Whatever full-size quit give up end result you sit up straight for reaching for your commercial employer, speak with the advantages of LinkedIn in Chapter one, it's viable on LinkedIn.

However, to permit effective growth, you want to stick to LinkedIn great practices due to the fact they may be important.

Thus, you should take it sluggish to recognize the practices referred to under. They are pivotal to you, your company, and its brand.

Determine Your Type of Content

Content is king. So, if you are not developing and posting content material fabric on LinkedIn, you want to begin now. As a agency, content material is an effective marketing and marketing method that is geared toward your centered customers – to stress them from the extent of recognition on the profits funnel to the element in which they purchase.

And with reference to posting content material fabric on LinkedIn, there are numerous provisions that you want to be privy to. Examined beneath are some of effective content material cloth fabric that you can run on LinkedIn.

Clickable Content: There are about three million customers on LinkedIn, a number of them are connects primarily based absolutely to your profile. If you're interested by drawing their interest for your LinkedIn profile, you need to put up content material fabric continuously. But is that automatic? No. We can wager that there may be some of them who might sincerely walk over your content material material possibly due to the fact your content material doesn't compel them to lean in and look.

The component then is that your content needs to be compelling and engaging. You can't have enough cash to be bland and boring nearly approximately content material fabric introduction on LinkedIn. Your connections have loads on their feeds already, whether or not or now not you will be given interest or now not relies upon on the way you gift what you are attempting to mention.

Can your content material fabric material push your readers to want to apprehend more in the subsequent net internet page? That's the essence of a clickable content material cloth.

One of the content cloth advertising and advertising techniques that makes this feasible is visible. Numbers from research indicated that visible content material cloth fabric are the most drivers on LinkedIn. So, if your content cloth consists of photos, animations, infographics, and loads of more, customers are much more likely to click on.

What are we pronouncing in summary? Avoid undeniable text. Black and white is not sufficient.

Another tip is to include a name-to-motion (CTA). Every reader has a behavior which you are trying to regulate and at the aspect on your content material material material marketing and advertising and marketing, you shouldn't omit the threat to reason them to take an motion. That's what CTA is set. If you don't tell them to click on on for extra or begin a free trial, they will be now not in all likelihood to suppose so themselves.

Identify Specific Audience: Being particular approximately target audience is one of the LinkedIn satisfactory practices that you have to encompass. As we've got instructed you earlier, anybody isn't always your intention. So, so long as you have got got a market place of interest, you need to understand people who belong to you and those who are not.

Within this identical body, you need to create content with the intention to enchantment in your particular target market. To advantage the insight that assist you to channel your content material to the proper people, you need to assess the usage of the following requirements:

• Who reads my content material material? Those who view and then you have a look at your content material are your audience. Face individuals who clicked via and direct your content cloth to them. Meanwhile, we are not pronouncing you need to neglect about about the possibility of gaining the attention of others. Our emphasis proper proper here is the want to realise who/what your priorities are.

● Who are my LinkedIn fanatics? It takes someone who is interested by your profile to study you. So, examine your fans. This is the manner you understand your crucial demographic institution.

● Who do I goal? Content is a marketing and advertising method to help you find out the ones you must reason the numerous crowd. Identify the ones you can goal and paintings toward growing the right content material fabric for them.

Stimulate Interests: Posting content fabric on LinkedIn due to the truth all people is doing so received't lead you or your employer everywhere. You actually have to be strategic collectively along with your effort. The second you recognize your dreams, you need to take a look at strategies on your content material creation technique. So, apart from using visuals, you need to now not fail at stimulating their interest. How do you try this?

• Post content material fabric that supply them perception about the corporation they belong to.

• Discuss subjects relevant to them.

• Ask questions normally. Make positive that the questions are the ones that could activate the, to want to find out more.

• Be enticing. High-degree of engagement is part of your CTA. Require them to percentage similar enjoy inside the statement segment, ask them to provide your pointers, and so forth.

Promote Industry-related Events: As the maximum essential social media community, there would possibly commonly be crowd-pulling agency-related sports making spherical. And for you, it makes real enjoy to talk about them. Meanwhile, don't really post and re-percentage, build conversations round them.

While you are selling the motive of the event, you could do little exposition at the difficulty through asking ability people what they sit up for getting to know. It's a way via which you can pique their interest. You can also moreover want to do this to your LinkedIn account or on the institution created for could-be people.

In phrases of content fabric cloth marketing, you could create content cloth in the course of the occasion. To try this correctly, the event wants to be associated with your emblem coverage.

Visual Appeal: As emphasized in previous bankruptcy, including media documents can be very inventive. This technique that even your font colour have to be attractive. Don't flip-off your goals with dull images, make certain any picture you operate accents the element you are trying to say in the next. You don't need to have a complicated photograph designing capabilities neither do you want to usually rent the service of 1. There are free operating photo gadget like Canva and Piktochart that you may use to create associated pix. All-in-all, make sure that your infographic is fairly practical and in-depth.

Career-Focused: Remember we said that developing relevant content material fabric fabric on your target audience is all you ought to do first. No industrial enterprise need to rush into throwing promotional portions inside the face of their goals. Except you create price first, don't sell. Of course, all of us recognize that a marketer has to sell. But to pays to reveal your desires that you care approximately them beyond what you are promoting. One of the tactics to do this is thru update of career-targeted content fabric. Doing this inside the body of the agency you percent with them will not most effective set up you as a thought-leader, however moreover as someone they may believe.

So, to your content, communicate approximately how matters artwork in understand to management, control, advertising and advertising, group-bonding, and upload links to open positions, if available.

Encourage Your Staff Members to Post Brand-Content

The personnel of any employer or organisation are its number one brand's image makers. Consequently, it's anticipated that a enterprise business company would optimize this. How do you optimize this?

• Make certain they be part of LinkedIn.

• Some of them ought to probable antagonize this flow into. So, don't strain them to reap this. All you need to do is help them recognize the benefit it brings to their personal private career increase. If need be, rent someone who is an professional on LinkedIn account control to manual them thru. And then, encourage them to use their presence to sell the emblem via posting emblem-targeted content on behalf of the company.

•   You can provide them with content material fabric introduction concept lists that speaks to your emblem. This is being recommended it's possible that some of them wouldn't realize what to position up.

•   Meanwhile, ensure they will be stored abreast of the activities of the commercial enterprise commercial enterprise enterprise.

•   And in the end, normally cope with them proper. When your employees are glad, it becomes much less hard for them to speak approximately you on social media net sites.

Optimize LinkedIn Pulse

Any industrial business enterprise that wants to revel in holistic reach, need to key into LinkedIn Pulse. This function lets in publishing of relevant content material cloth. Unlike what you put up in your LinkedIn profile, what are the advantages of LinkedIn Pulse?

- Improved and targeted focused on for the reason that your content will obtain does that it subjects to and ultimately, you get to evaluate the demographic factors of your goals.

- When your guide gets immoderate social shares, you end up a pinnacle rating thru Pulse. You can recollect what this indicates in your agency or emblem.

- With LinkedIn Pulse, you've got a chance to create contents with back links. This brings you numerous search engine advertising advantages.

- Like regular weblog sports established with the useful resource of your enterprise corporation, you can tag content material cloth material for your e-book. What's the implication of this? Your searchability will boom and also you experience severa blessings over and over all yet again while you seem on SERPs.

• Content advertising and marketing and advertising is a method commonplace to most organizations. At least, the ones on-line. This manner that there are extra than enough content fabric for on-line clients to cope with. As a result of this, content material material advertising is quite aggressive. LinkedIn pulse is an possibility to conquer this opposition.

Now, how do you beat the competition?

1. Create content fabric that is inner a thousand phrases restriction.

2. Make fine it has a exquisite headline.

3. Focus on organization/career trouble subjects.

four. Include media files such photos, motion snap shots, animations, and infographics.

5. Avoid content material fabric cloth that include influencers.

Remain Active

Let's put it this manner: our degree of activeness impacts your visibility on line. So, you want to live lively. When you grow to be inactive, you kill the hobby of your enthusiasts. If you need to collect be given as actual with and followership, you want to spend fantastic time on LinkedIn. Because we apprehend it isn't always clean developing content material fabric fabric usually within the course of the day, you have to do the subsequent that lets in you to live applicable on LinkedIn.

• Post as a minimum as quickly as in a day. If you could do extra, first-class. We suggest that you have your posting schedule earlier than or after agency hours.

• Be enticing. Like posts, bypass observation when you have a few detail reasonable to mention, and we suggest that you be a part of companies.

• Continually replace your capabilities, business employer data, cover images, and others.

• Incorporate movement photographs. If pictures ought to mention more than one thousand phrases, how a good deal more a video?

• Post hobby openings and scholarship opportunities.

• Let you readers and fanatics see you as human. Businesses having social media web sites seems absurd but so long as you'll be human, you may win. Be in conversations, be real, show love on your lovers – desire them happy birthday, re-percent their useful posts too, and so forth.

Use LinkedIn Analytics to Track Your Success

Being able to degree your fulfillment on LinkedIn is ideal specially at the same time as you want to execute content material advertising strategies that generate consequences. To gain insights regarding your efforts, the metrics highlighted under are important:

• Visitor Demography: Through this, you may find out who reads your content material material. Once you note their list, you can find out their assignment description, corporation, vicinity, diploma, business enterprise's body of workers period, function, and so forth.

• Views: Over a particular time body, you get to look how many people considered your employer's net internet page.

• Impression: This refers to the quantity of instances your content fabric became confirmed to LinkedIn clients.

• Click: This refers to the numbers of time LinkedIn users clicked on the selection of your organization, the logo, name, or content material material.

• Follower: This lets you understand the quantity of fanatics you received from a subsidized publish.

• Engagement: This describes the style of impressions which has been divided with the aid of the interactions which LinkedIn customers have along side your posts.

- Audience: Your purpose marketplace describes individuals who appeared your placed up. You get to recognize whether or no longer it's viewed via each of your followers or certainly a particular segment.

Getting More Results Using LinkedIn

As a advertising expert, you will be anticipated to use all of the LinkedIn assets at your disposal to make things work. There can be masses so you can use. So, if your organisation isn't always on LinkedIn, now is the time. However, you want to pay interest no longer to abuse the assets at your disposal. What are we pronouncing? You want to be human whilst the usage of the device made to be had to you.

For example, if you want to ensure your goals view your placed up, you need to create contents that you might be inclined to engage with yourself. And make sure something you placed up relates well with the focal point and reason of your enterprise.

LinkedIn Mistakes That You Should Avoid

Once another time, be reminded that About LinkedIn, 2019 well-knownshows that there are approximately 610 million users at the platform. Also, there are about 10 million lively approach posts available at the platform. Without doubt, that is the tremendous professional social media internet internet page each person with the motive of professional profession growth must belong to.

But lots of oldsters which might be energetic on one-of-a-kind social media web sites like Facebook, Instagram, and Twitter keep away from LinkedIn because of the reality they assume it's complicated. And they're proper. On LinkedIn, a easy mistake or inattention want to placed a dent in your authenticity as a professional. Thus, you need to be careful about your sports activities on LinkedIn. So, what are the mistakes you must avoid on LinkedIn?

Not Creating Thorough Goals

As a marketer, don't forget about about the want to have truly stated goals on LinkedIn. Setting desires is your ultimate guide to optimizing some time at the platform and ensuring some detail you do there can be in reality properly well worth it.

In order to benefit your goals, you have to spend incredible effort and time on LinkedIn connecting with similar minds which includes you. However, don't be in a rush. The reality which you were told that LinkedIn allows your profession and business, doesn't suggest it's a magic.

You want to spend time constructing your profile as valuable. What can the headhunters who're searching for new skills remove out of your profile? Does your profile them? Are your studies and skills visible and precious sufficient? Do you stand as someone who can assist them remedy the demanding situations of their commercial enterprise?

When you create a radical purpose to your LinkedIn profile, it turns into less hard to get it right and gain proper give up result inside a short time period.

Your Profile Does Not Pronounce Your Expertise

Some LinkedIn customers are on the platform to in particular headhunt for raw talents on behalf in their business corporation. They are in the enterprise enterprise of evaluating profiles. Thus, it's important which you set up your profile to pronounce precisely what you do.

There are skills for putting in profiles to reflect the amount of your facts. The preference is yours to fill your profile up with the desired information or now not.

So, skip lower once more now on your LinkedIn account. Does it completely mirror your educational information, enjoy, and capabilities? Is it okay to even name your LinkedIn profile a virtual resume? Yes.

Don't be careless or lazy, it's less complex to be judged with the aid of manner of manner of your horrible grammar and punctuation in black and white. After all, it's far anticipated which you should have taken it slow to check and re-check.

Find brief pointers beneath:

- Have a catchy headline.

- Create compelling profile summary.

- Post content relevant for your brand and agency.

- Consistently make it clean that you are a professional on your problem.

You Share Too Personal Events

Although LinkedIn is likewise a social media internet site, it's designed with purpose for specialists. Thus, you have to be cautious now not put up subjects which might be deemed too private. Unlike Facebook or Instagram, you can't show off your new automobile or add a video of you taking your canine for a walk.

When it entails content material introduction, you need to be cautious now not to percentage incorrect opinions or unfounded claims. These movements are so unprofessional. LinkedIn is not your non-public diary in that you write secrets and techniques and techniques and techniques nor is it a playground in that you communicate lousily without care.

Whether in your wall or in companies, you ought to avoid arguments that lack intellectual base, avoid call-calling, among others. Keep lawsuits to your self, you are in all likelihood not going to comply with the whole thing that's shared on LinkedIn; and it's okay. Just be tolerant. If you can't show tolerance in a virtual area, how do you convince your would possibly-be employee that the case may also need to unique while you in the long run get recruited via way in their organization?

Anything that would shy away headhunters while discovered want to be resisted.

Not Improving Your LinkedIn

Imagine a state of affairs in that you sooner or later get the pastime you have got been seeking out via LinkedIn. Before you bought the system, you constantly comply with the pointers recommended within the previous chapters. And then, you obtain the interest and the bankruptcy to being seen on LinkedIn changed into closed. This is a tremendous mistake which you need to keep away from.

One element is real: You aren't going to be at the pastime all the time. Whether due to process dissatisfaction or the thirst for a profession growth, you might need to eventually depart your gift assignment. So, in which do you come to while you need to raise your ladder? You move again to LinkedIn again, right?

The message is which you need to in no way forget approximately your LinkedIn account. Keep it updated with the proper content material. Stay relevant in your selected enterprise. Learn new talents, get new certification, and replace them for your profile. When you continuously replace your profile, you turn out to be strategically positioned at the identical time as opportunities higher than the handiest you have got in the long run seem.

Don't wait until you're seeking out such opportunities earlier than you start updating.

There is a warning notwithstanding the truth that. Don't located up an excessive amount of. Always, the best of content material cloth surpasses the amount.

Neglecting Your Network

There isn't always any element in following all of the techniques for optimizing LinkedIn that we have got given you and developing the right connections only that allows you to in the end forget about approximately them.

You need to stay energetic. Even despite the reality that we've got were given counseled you in competition to posting an excessive amount of, you must optimize your presence via turning into a member of organization-associated corporations. Once you're capable of amass industry-associated connections, you want to govern what you have got were given a great manner to increase your legitimacy and genuineness.

Mind you, don't be too brief to ship income message or request for favors for your connections. Develop real relationships first.

Forgetting Keywords

Keywords are critical to optimizing your presence on-line. If you need to get determined on LinkedIn, along with key terms on your profile is 2d to none. When you have were given the key phrases related to your corporation inside the proper place —

headline, assignment description, and profile summary, it'll be less complex to be located at the same time as headhunters use the search engine.

Let's assume that your advertising and advertising specialization is content fabric writing, you need to use keywords together with article, search engine marketing content material material material, and content cloth cloth advertising and marketing and advertising. These key phrases allow you to tank pinnacle in the are seeking for consequences made available with the aid of way of LinkedIn to the searcher.

Not Requesting for Help

You don't understand it all and that's no longer a criminal offense. It's most effective a crime in case you fail to ask questions. As a amateur, you could grow to be neglecting the information which you should include into your profile.

Thus, even at the same time as you're excessive great you've got ticked all the sections, you want to are looking for for the assist of a second eyes. We endorse that you are searching for for the assist of someone who is familiar with how LinkedIn works. On a second word, the individual may be a person in your employer who is additionally an expert LinkedIn patron.

And don't be too non-public whilst you growing your profile. You want to thrive to head away an extended-lasting have an impact on on your profile traffic, so craft your tale find it irresistible's about them and not you. So, rather than surely talking about your instructional statistics, highlight the competencies that you have acquired. Highlight how those skills have to assist you serve the organization or agency you are targeting, among others.

Chapter 6: Creating the Content That Attracts on LinkedIn

Have you stopped to ask yourself the form of content you would like to study if you have been to your desires' shoes? We are requesting you to do this as it's greater or less a fruitless try if your content material doesn't talk or resonate inside the mind of your goals. Besides. What's the aspect if a content material does no longer assist you optimize your visibility?

As you evaluate your content advertising efforts so far, have it in the back of your thoughts that each content fabric you positioned up in this expert social media website online will bypass a protracted manner to make or mar your brand constructing, whether or not or no longer private or corporate.

In this chapter, we're able to take you via the strategies you could set up in developing the proper content material fabric. So, what are the forms of content cloth that you may optimize for your platform?

Blogs

The Ultimate List of Digital Marketing Statistics, 2019, well-knownshows that over 80% of social media or cutting-edge entrepreneurs who use blog posts have a excessive go back from their marketing and advertising and advertising funding.

So, as you may see, strolling a blog is one of the methods through which your emblem can gain many goal market at a time. If you're planning to expand your community on LinkedIn and function your company as an professional, jogging a weblog is a step in the proper course.

With LinkedIn publishing platform, you can post weblog content material wealthy in applicable information that customers and corporations cannot flip their eyes a long way from.

Meanwhile, earlier than you begin to blog you have to create a reason to your on foot a weblog. Your aim should one or more of the subsequent:

- Educating

- Informing, and

- Entertaining.

You also can comprise enjoyment into your blogs. Don't ? But then, you ought to do that with the focus of your business enterprise behind your mind. When it comes to teaching and informing, you can write professional opinion and evaluation or percent the ones supplied through the usage of the use of authorities to your enterprise. Well, you don't need to be share proper now. You can use link building to cite the government on your employer. Be reminded that hyperlink constructing is part of the techniques for rating on SERPs. All you want to do is ensure it's applicable to what you are speakme about on your blog positioned up.

The styles of blog content material that you can percent as weblog via LinkedIn are:

- Opinion articles

- Guest writers

- Contribution of government to conversations.

- How-to content material cloth

- Flash memories

- Listicles

- Ultimate guides

- Newsworthy content material cloth

Images

Don't take as a right the importance of snap shots. Not best are snap shots price-powerful, they're furthermore time-maintaining.

But proper right here is the caution – don't use pix for the sake of doing so. Make certain something image you operate resonates collectively with your goals. Don't get it incorrect although. Also, make certain it offers aesthetic charge - that is, it want to be visually appealing.

In addition, encompass capture descriptions and storyline round snap shots particularly if it's an photograph of your product. Even the photo need to be saved with the proper key phrases earlier than you placed up online. Every description you ascribe to images want to consist of the right key phrases as properly.

We recognize that it is not that clean to create and put up prolonged seo content material, so sense loose to percentage concept-stimulating photographs in your LinkedIn page.

So, what are the types of snap shots you may use on LinkedIn?

• Lifestyle snap shots

• Pictures from enterprise-associated photographs

• Products

- Cartoons

- Memes

- GIFs

Infographics

Never underestimate the strength of infographics. In fact, infographics rank higher than blogs. With infographics, you could present studies results on your goals, you may deliver illustrative examples, amongst others. It's a time-speakme way to keep your LinkedIn profile lively in case you don't have lots time at your disposal.

Like snap shots and easy visuals, traffic are interested in infographics. With infographics you get oneway links which you didn't even request for.

In addition, with infographics, it's much less tough to consist of CTAs.

White Papers and Case Studies

White papers and case research is a expert and agency manner to promote your emblem. What is a white paper and a case have a look at? White paper is a file which facts studies about your area or employer on the same time as case look at is a more unique and in-depth research. In order terms, at the same time as white paper is substantial, case study is targeted on a particular event.

What roles do those play in respect in your advertising approach?

• White paper permits to showcase the strategic function of a agency inside the region at the same time as emphasizing the records, creativity, reap, and information of the organization.

• Case have a have a have a look at showcases in clear terms the method and strategies utilized in starting up, negotiating, executing, and evaluating a task via the use of a agency in a given zone.

However, you shouldn't certainly consist of those into your content fabric advertising and marketing technique because all people else is doing so. Before you do, make certain something is contained therein is confirmed, proofread, and informative sufficient. Avoid irrelevant information that would rub a dent of unprofessionalism in your brand or organization. Remember you may be imparting white papers and case research maximum of the time that allows you to set up a connection with your dreams, so do it well. At least, if it's well truly worth doing.

Avoid bluffs. Abstain from boasting. And encompass simplest statistics and vital data. And don't overlook to embody the records of your enterprise, the achievements, and diploma of customers' loyalty.

What more do you stand to benefit from white papers and case research?

• White papers and case research make contributions substantially for your weblog internet website.

- They assist you to draw antique and new desires.

- They deliver a lift to customers' loyalty.

- They generate viable leads.

- You can post them to your LinkedIn net net web page with CTAs covered into them.

Video

Thanks to the revolution of virtual age. With proper interest to element, all people can create video and percentage with their connections on LinkedIn. You can do that to your profile, web page updates, or LinkedIn author.

Besides, constant with Walters, 2015, about 75% of online site visitors is earned via using video updates alone.

Meanwhile, you don't definitely create video due to the fact each person is doing it. If you need to create video, you need to stand out. Ensure that your video has the proper aesthetic, clear tones, useful idea, and excessive-level engagement.

Also, you need to do your terrific to create instructing, interesting, and informative video content material material in case you are ready to do this. You don't need to create content material cloth material as a way to placed a dent on your logo. Not only must it represent the image of your logo well, it should as it should be cater for the desires of your target audience.

It's an funding in your component, so don't waste your property without a move returned.

Webinars

Webinars are people to people stay occasions. Usually, it takes the form of interactive consultation among a logo and its site visitors on a given platform. During the session individuals could have interplay and additionally initiate chats.

According to Nguyen, 2015, check found that approximately 40% of webinar attendees commonly change into leads. Many enterprise organization entrepreneurs are embracing webinar because it gives them the possibility to place a face and human voice within the returned of its brand and experience pinnacle remarks from dreams.

If you haven't covered webinar into your advertising and advertising and marketing techniques, now's the time to take your chance through LinkedIn with the resource of promoting your webinar and using prolonged traffic on your net net web page. On LinkedIn, quite some human beings and specialists are keen to investigate, absolutely so they join up for webinars in which they will have interaction with professionals and specialists of their organisation.

Podcasts and Audio

Podcast or audio is superb beneficial aid which your organization can use to construct a strong LinkedIn community. If you would like to enjoy persisted interplay and excessive stage engagement, podcast or audio is ideal for you.

Gibbs, 2019, well-knownshows that about 90% of podcast and audio subscribers are reliable to the emblem whose content material they pay interest.

So, the key is to create collection of podcast and audio with thoughts-blowing content material cloth. It's essential to supply them with quality content if you really want to assemble a community of dedicated followers. Give them what they love and that they gained't save you being devoted to you.

Despite the plenty of statistics that flood us each day, a few virtual clients though leave out out. So, you could channel your podcast or audio into preserving them informed about newsworthy occasion on your organization. Links in your podcast or audio may be located on your LinkedIn profile or attached to a seen.

Downloadables

Materials which includes eBooks, closing courses, templates, record, and the manner-to, among others, which you supply for your goals in exchange for his or her emails are what we refer to downloadables.

Downloadables are one of the strategies to construct an electronic mail listing organically in assessment to having to shop for one.

How do you get them to grant you're their e mail? Those equipped to enjoy the content material cloth of your fabric, eBook as an instance, is probably required to enter their email in a field just so the cloth might be sent to them. Or, they might be required to create an account the usage of their e mail deal with and password in advance than they could download the content material cloth material.

You also can percent the hyperlink to any downloadable in your LinkedIn. Get prepared to draw a big internet web page site visitors similarly to generate leads if the content material fabric fabric is relevant for your target audience.

Factors To Consider Before Choosing Your Type of Content

Apart from deciding on the shape of channels to push your content fabric fabric via, it's far critical to understand your emblem and choose the type of content material fabric that's appropriate for you.

Five factors need to be considered in advance than selecting your sort of content. They were examined underneath:

- Know your purpose: Creating content material on LinkedIn isn't always some element you leap into due to the reality clearly each person is doing it. You need to have a aim an remarkable way to deliver your content material a path. So, in advance than you start, ask your self: What do I want to obtain with this content material material?

- Responsive Audience: Before you bypass earlier to create post, make certain about the type of content material so that it will stimulate response from your intention marketplace. You don't want to create content material fabric that your goals gained't interact.

- Your Platform: No depend the kind of fanatics and connections you have on any social platform, no longer all of them is wholesome for your content cloth. You need to check which amongst them may be receiving your content the most inside the light of what your aim is.

- Social media: Will it is easy to post the content material you create on social media structures?

- Resources: It's now not surely beneficial to leap into content material material advertising and marketing because of the truth your opposition is doing so. Even if you decided to, you don't need to do what they're doing. What you have to ask your self first is when you have the wished assets. By assets, we advocate talents, coins, and human functionality that is probably required to always create incredible posts, video, images, podcasts, and webinars, among others.

Above all, you shouldn't demotivate your objectives or enthusiasts because of posting dull content material cloth. Spice it up, don't comply with one manner to doing it. Diversity is in truth important if you need to benefit a far broader goal market without a barrier.

Effective use of Content Marketing

As a result of its based technique to content advertising and marketing and advertising and marketing, maximum clients pick out LinkedIn to Twitter. Thus, time past regulation, it has grown because the center of enterprise-focused content material promoting.

However, irrespective of its developing use, LinkedIn customers though don't forget a sure question. The question is if surely all content material cloth earnings the equal degree of visibility?

Realistically, it's now not constantly possible to get the popular degree of visibility. But does that suggest employer entrepreneurs have to forego their content material fabric advertising efforts? The solution is NO.

Remember we best stated gaining the same stage of visibility isn't always typically feasible. This approach that entrepreneurs can emerge as seen to their desires inside the event that they live active on LinkedIn. We have earlier mentioned the need to be active on-line as an character, logo, or agency.

Guide For LinkedIn Content Marketing Plan

The kind of content material advertising you're doing is based upon on the platform you're aiming at. Above all else, developing the kind of platform that your objectives can relate with is the maximum important.

Since LinkedIn is a platform created for stakeholders in industries, you need to create the shape of content material material that will help you gain their hobby.

And there can be no distinctive way to it than growing the content material cloth that resonate with your aim market to three expert diploma. You are already conscious that LinkedIn is the one of the structures that provide you with industry results related to the purpose of your agency. Among different things, with the right content fabric advertising and marketing method, you may advantage dependable leads and decorate the quantity of engagement you've got got.

Meanwhile, one terrific characteristic which you want to research is being affected individual on the identical time as geared up. It doesn't depend whether or not or not all of the content fabric advertising recommendations available, you need to be willing to permit the improvement take region without being in haste.

A lot of things make LinkedIn unique from one-of-a-kind social media structures. For instance, you want endorsement from specialists who're authority in your business enterprise for talents which you have included to your profile. Imagine if the managing director of an global financial business enterprise endorses your capability as a economic advertising and advertising representative?

Owing to a number of these placing versions, you need to have a content material fabric marketing and advertising and marketing technique that meet the identical vintage of B2B and B2C expected on LinkedIn. You do not have anything to worry approximately even though as there are content material fabric advertising and marketing device that you could use to set your self up for achievement. For instance, show off and organisation agency pages are the competencies that permit the creation of carrier control on the same time as InMail and associated talents facilitate the emblem reputation sports activities of companies.

Like we've got brought you to a few types of content material cloth earlier, you can increase the authority of your agency thru webinars, company-related occasions, and eBooks, among others. And if you are interested in advertising and marketing, using subsidized posts feature is important.

More than some issue, those functions are beneficial for connecting with goals. Although the improvement also can exceptional be measurable at a slow pace, you could constantly get consequences which may be terrific.

To assist you via this technique, there are sure steps that your industrial corporation agency can comply with. Some of the steps are considered beneath:

Focus on Your Network Growth

By now, you need to have understood that LinkedIn is unique. Although it's a social media net website online on line, you ought to no longer overlook that it's designed with an cause for professionals. So, your approach wants to range.

Ordinarily, you may start through sending invitations to folks who percent the identical hobby with you. That's the most commonplace technique which anybody can use without stress.

Other easy techniques consist of sending customized message requesting for connection. To try this, make sure you:

•   Have an in depth profile internet page.

•   Be an active customer at the agencies you belong to.

•   Attach your e mail signature to the LinkedIn URL.

Having been purchased via manner of Microsoft, the internet website online boasts of about 610 million clients. What are you able to do with this shape of users? You can create a massive community for your self amongst these customers through publishing content material material on the platform, and doing so constantly.

Creation of Company Page

In a preceding bankruptcy, you learnt about the way to set-up a web web page to your business enterprise. If your agency is still with out a business enterprise net net page, you ought to gain this right away. Follow the instructions carefully and don't hesitate to invite question if you aren't certain. Without a enterprise internet net page, there may be no way you may set up your agency as an authority.

Apart from supplying facts approximately the identity of your business enterprise, its nature, technique of operating, you shouldn't forget about about to feature the emblem of your business enterprise. You must create one if in any respect your agency has none however.

You ought to moreover recognize that on the identical time as the internet web page offers facts about the business company, it's additionally the manner with the aid of which you percent content material that complements the visibility of your emblem.

Once you have got got a organisation web page, it becomes less tough to get at some stage in to your enthusiasts. You need to have written down your content material thoughts and understand your time table. The subjects that you may write on primarily based in your enterprise encompass:

• Trends

• Business associated advises/guidelines

• Newsfeed from the company

• Valid opinion given through the usage of authorities on your organisation.

Focused Content Marketing

Your content material material marketing need to be targeted. What's the cause of creating content fabric on LinkedIn even as there is no course or cause? Generally, your content want to educate, encourage, or entertain. Wherever your commercial employer choose to face, it want to led through a motive or desires. Among exceptional subjects, you have to do the following with content cloth advertising:

● Publish authentic facts – It's crucial which you appearance past the want to incorporate income merchandising into your content. While it's a supply and take scenario, you need to be willing to provide extra. Publish helpful records in your agency's web web page. You can share business enterprise updates and occasions with them, introduce them to on-line courses – loose or paid, and masses of greater.

● Be interesting: Your goal has more than sufficient content material fabric to address. Do they want extra? No. What then do they need? They the kind of content material fabric that hobbies them. They are not asking you to reveal your content material material to a few form of jokes, truely that they want you to make it exciting to have a look at. Add some a laugh, encompass animation, images, use cartoons in driving domestic your element, and plenty of greater.

• Don't be egocentric: It's good enough to recognition on developing your internet net page however don't be egocentric. Other pages are trying to do the equal element as nicely. Post applicable comments on their posts, like, and percentage if you find it beneficial. When you show others that you can notice theirs, they may also be aware of you.

• Be engaging: The diploma of engagement which customers have with your content cloth topics plenty. At each thing in the development of your content material fabric, ensure you get your goal market involved. Spur them to have interaction you within the remark section and be there to reply. Don't sincerely positioned up and depart. Be there after they start responding.

Create a Plan this is Specific to the Newsfeed

Important records approximately your organisation or the company you belong to are anticipated to be made to be had for your newsfeed. Apart from that you could additionally preserve them updated approximately process possibilities for your company.

You can lease the pointers under to manual you in appealing customers via your newsfeed:

•   Share applicable information approximately to be had mission possibilities.

•   Introduce them to abilties they are able to learn how to enhance their possibilities for task possibilities to your company or enterprise.

•   Hint them on the profession possibilities they might benefit from your employer.

To have extraordinary impact, you need to create a design for the content that you want to be sharing in your newsfeed. Not only will doing so offer you with a sense of route, you benefit a legitimate role in the thoughts of your customers. Eventually, they may see your page as in which they could get superb information associated with the industry.

Be Selective with Groups Membership

You don't need to belong to each employer that comes your way on LinkedIn. Before you be part of a collection, ensure it's crucial and relevant for your market location of interest.

There might be loads of corporations besides, you definitely want to deliberate and intentional. But how need to make the right choice even as you don't comprehend what you're looking out for? So we advise which you select out together with your desires first.

Once you be part of a set that could offer benefits along side boosting your visibility and developing the site visitors on your net page, you want to additionally take part within the activities of the employer.

You must be willing to percent thoughts and information as well. Don't keep anything that would help human beings of your organization to your self.

What need to you do earlier than you be a part of a set?

- Check the sort of customers.

- Check the volume of engagement which takes area a number of the participants.

Find the information difficulty that gives you critical facts approximately a set earlier than you be a part of. For the quantity of engagement amongst individuals, see the large type of posts in the previous month. This comes with variety of feedback underneath every placed up.

Keep Personal Thoughts To Yourself

LinkedIn is not your traditional social media web internet websites. If you need to percent connections with professionals, you should furthermore act like a professional. How do you display which you are a expert? Your articles and feedback want to accessory this. Your private thoughts and messages must be saved to your self.

It doesn't depend what your intentions are, LinkedIn is not a platform in which you brag about your new residence, the meal you had at a eating place, or your new dressmaker shoe.

Learn Patience

LinkedIn isn't your normal social media platform. So, you can't usually get the results you're eager to see. Learn endurance. Embrace this smooth reality in order now not to prevent your regular boom at the platform. There may be times in which the volume of engagement collectively collectively together with your put up can even be underneath your expectancies. It doesn't recommend you are not pronouncing the right trouble, it doesn't even suggest you are not developing. Expectations won't be completed due to the fact you in all likelihood don't percentage the same time zones collectively together with your clients.

It takes time —it's gradual, however you need to live visible. And don't permit or now not it's approximately your net web page on my own. Attend to the goals of others as well.

Make applicable feedback even at the posts of your competition.

Schedule Your Updates

You need to be careful on the aspect of your approach to uploading on LinkedIn. You don't ought to placed up all the time, save you uploading the same information over and over yet again.

What works on unique structures may likely absolutely grow to be giving your horrible effects on LinkedIn. You acquired't need to be tagged a spammer. While your updates have to be relevant on your industry, you want to offer sparkling perspective in every replace. Plus, you don't need to put up every hours of the day. Keep it to one or and your internet net page is probably first-class. And if you have nothing to feature, spend it sluggish reading the posts of others and commenting on them.

Keep it without delay and short

Don't pressure your clients into some bottomless pit at the equal time as you put up. Be immediately to the aspect and avoid beside the issue information. This subjects in case you need them to engage together with your posts. Apart from being applicable, you need be at once. How do you're making this feasible?

- Use titles.

- Use self-explanatory subheadings.

- Use bullet factors or numbering.

Getting Headlining Right

Making fine your dreams have a take a look at your content fabric even as it appears in their newsfeeds starts offevolved with having the proper headline. Not first-class need to your headline be accurate, it want to be captivating enough to guide them to want to have a take a look at to the stop.

Be Consistent

To be seen on LinkedIn, you need to be normal. What's the detail for disaster on LinkedIn? Being active for a day and turning into no-in which-to-be-determined for an entire week. You need to be regular together with your updates.

While we recommend in competition to posting almost each hours of the day, it's good enough to position up as soon as in an afternoon.

Optimize LinkedIn Publishing Platform

You stand to advantage lots whilst you operate LinkedIn publishing platform. Important among them is the possibility to attain your target market without pressure as long as your content is relevant.

Even LinkedIn can decide to annotate your paintings, percent it in addition to sell its advert region on the internet web page of your content fabric.

Incorporate the Use of SlideShare

Your eBooks and blogs won't usually meet your set expectancies. You can then use distinct characteristic like SlideShare which LinkedIn gives. SlideShare lets you upload seen content to your content material material with out a trouble.

How do you do this? You should have created a web page for your employer on LinkedIn, then link the SlideShare net page to company's internet page. Once you do that, every document you create on SlideShare may be proven for your LinkedIn account.

But you should have included the right seen content material material that could appeal to immoderate-degree interaction. We are but to see everyone whose senses don't have interaction with a properly created seen. The content material cloth can be a simplification of a subject of hobby on your enterprise. What subjects is clarity and high-quality seen.

Chapter 7: Setting Up Your LinkedIn Company Page

To sell your emblem on LinkedIn, you need a full-blown enterprise page. The enterprise employer web page is a professional manner to permit LinkedIn customers have a look at your logo, your merchandise, your organization company, similarly to undertaking possibilities that your business enterprise gives.

Although the employer agency pages had been regularly used as HR landing pages, now, this platform gives a splendid possibility for growing emblem recognition and selling]your services to functionality customers.

In order to set up a employer page, you want an energetic LinkedIn private profile first. Assuming that you have one, honestly take a look at the subsequent steps to create the page for your organisation.

Step #1: Add Your Company

Go to https://enterprise organization.Linkedin.Com/marketing and advertising-answers/linkedin-pages and click on on 'Create Your Page'. Enter the decision of your commercial enterprise company and provide you with a URL to be able to assist human beings locate your internet net web page. Note that you can not alternate the URL later, so ensure to choose appropriately. Then, test the checkbox to verify which you are an right consultant of the organisation and click on on on 'Create Page'.

The shell is robotically created. To start building your internet web page, truly click on at the 'Get Started' button.

Step #2: Add Your Image

Upload your logo (3 hundred x 3 hundred pixels recommended) as your profile photograph, and upload a cover image (ideally 1536 x 768 px) to provide a glimpse of what your business enterprise business enterprise is prepared. Keep in mind that organizations with logos have greater visitors, so do now not be tempted to skip this step.

Step #3: Create Your Description

LinkedIn lets in you to use 2,000 characters in your description, but be conscious that it's far the primary 156 terms that appear to your commercial business enterprise organisation internet web page's preview this is displayed on Google, so ensure to write down an high-quality beginning.

You have the option to feature 20 specialties. Think of them as keywords advert they could help people discover your company on LinkedIn, so make certain to represents the energy and understanding of your commercial employer right here.

Step #4: Your Company's Details

Here, you'll enter the location of your agency, your internet net page's URL, your business enterprise, duration and type of your employer, in addition to different critical facts that describe your enterprise corporation.

Step #five: Publish the Page

To go stay, click on on 'Publish'. Before you preserve, it is advocated to test what the corporation net net web page looks as if at the same time as one-of-a-kind customers click on it. To check it out, click on 'Member View'. If you aren't happy the arrival of your net web page, go to 'Manage Page' and make a few adjustments.

Step #6: Page Administrators

If you are not making plans to run your LinkedIn company corporation internet web page by myself, then you could want to pick the human beings which can administer the web page.

To add extra employees, click on on at the 'Me' button discovered on the pinnacle of your net internet page. Then, visit 'Manage', choose your Company Page. There, pick out 'Admin Tools' □ 'Page Admins'. Then, input the decision of the humans you want to offer access to the net page.

Note: You need to already be related to those people on LinkedIn as a way to choose them as administrators.

Chapter 8: The Perfect Strategy

Simply developing a business business employer internet page doesn't imply that the right connections will come your manner. Just like with every other platform, you want to have a brilliant advertising and marketing and marketing approach for LinkedIn as nicely. Here is what you could do in case you need to decorate your hazard for success:

Create a Showcase Page

Showcase pages are the proper way to reveal off a specific a part of your organisation which you are most glad with. This is a tremendous possibility to place the highlight on your excellent product and entice capability customers.

The show off pages paintings as some form of subdomains to your corporation internet internet page, and having you could truely sincerely make a difference as LinkedIn customers also can follow them separately if they will be in particular interested by a specific services or products. You could have up to showcase pages.

To create one, click on on the 'Me' button, and under 'Manage', choose your Company Page. Then, go to 'Admin Tools' □ 'Create a Showcase Page'.

Have Your Employees Connected

Your largest advocates on LinkedIn are your employees. Having them as followers way which you have get entry to to their networks and connections, that can notably growth your acquire and convey more site site visitors for your Company Page. Encourage your employees to be related together together along with your Company Page to growth logo cognizance.

Keep Followers Informed

The first-rate way to enhance your intention marketplace is to maintain the one you have had been given glad. Make certain to often placed up valuable content fabric which encompass articles, weblog posts, or special updated in your enterprise. Also, if you may bear in mind an outside article that may be valuable in your fans, do not hesitate to location up it as properly.

Choose LinkedIn Groups

LinkedIn Groups offer a super manner that allows you to connect to people out of your region which may be outside of your right away circle. Being active in a LinkedIn Group and attractive in discussions can energy greater website on-line site visitors on your Page.

Want to discover a Group in order to suit your reason? You can test out some LinkedIn suggestions with the 'Group Discover' preference, or in reality use the hunt bar in case you apprehend what you are looking for.

Go Global

If you've got were given clients in some international locations wherein English is not the valid language, then you definately simply certainly can also need to consider adding an outline of your business enterprise written in considered one of a kind languages. Don't fear, you don't want to rent a translator for that purpose. LinkedIn offers multi-language gear that can contend with this for you.

Publish on the Right Times

Just just like the techniques to your one-of-a-kind platforms, your LinkedIn publishing ought to additionally be planned for. LinkedIn research says that the high-quality time for content material material fabric publishing on LinkedIn is in the morning and after business business enterprise hours. This is at the same time as people are the most engaged, so that you could probable need to take gain of this statistics and time desk your put up for then.

Chapter 9: Advertising on LinkedIn

If you want to intention your message to wonderful professionals, whether or not or now not CEOs or influencers, then marketing on LinkedIn is really some element you should take advantage of. Once you decide what you want to put it up for sale and who is your purpose market, then you could preserve with the following steps.

Step #1: Your 'Campaign Manager' Account

First of all, to start, you need to have a 'Campaign Manager' account, which you may address right right here https://www.Linkedin.Com/advert-beta/login. This is a tool that lets in you manage and optimize your commercials in the maximum handy manner possible. Plus, this device gives some beneficial device which will show the general performance of your advertisements, in order that's an introduced bonus.

Step #2: Choose the Type of Your Ad

Next, you need to pick the sort of advert you want to sell. There are 3 alternatives available:

1.Sponsored Content

2.Text Ads

3.Sponsored InMail

You can also create your campaign with all of the three codecs to make sure the most feasible gain.

Once you select the form of advert, input the decision of your marketing campaign, pick out out the language of your target market, and choose the decision-to-motion possibility, that is available first-rate for the Sponsored-Content commercials.

Step #three: Create the Ad

The extraordinary detail about the Campaign Manager is that it walks you via the steps of creation, imparting you pointers and help alongside the manner. Follow the stairs choosing the alternatives that fit your purpose the maximum.

Step #4: Target the Ad

At this factor, ensure that your advert could be focused to the proper people. You want to specify some necessities along with location, college names, company names, degree, challenge name, gender, age, years of revel in, talents, and so on. Make high quality to shop your standards, so you can tempo topics up the subsequent time you choice to promote it on LinkedIn.

Step #5: Set the Budget and Schedule

There are three methods in which you could pay for the commercials:

1.Cost Per Click (CPC)

2.Cost Per Impression (CPM) – for the messages in a member's view

3.Cost Per Send – for the Sponsored InMail classified ads (right right here, you pay high-quality for those messages which can be received)

For the CPM and CPS choice, you're allowed to set a maximum each day budget you are inclined to spend, and a bid price.

After that, in reality time desk the begin and stop date and time for the advert, and also you're carried out.

Is Your Marketing Strategy Working?

If you're pulling your metrics from some other social media platform, you then definately are probably lacking out at the actual picture of your LinkedIn ordinary performance. The remarkable manner to check in case your marketing and advertising and advertising and marketing technique is running, is through manner of finding out the built-in analytics device on LinkedIn.

Go to the toolbar fount on the top of your internet page and click on at the 'Analytics' button. You will see that there are three available options:

Visitors - This is wherein records at the individuals who visit your page is stored. Here you may see the overall observe of page view, the web site visitors metrics, you can isolate facts from a selected time and date, see statistics from high-quality pages in your profile, further to peer unique information of the those who view your web page (interest function, place, company, and so forth.)

Updates – Here you could find records about the content cloth you proportion. These engagement metrics embody the impressions, clicks, stocks, likes, clicks, and so forth.

Followers – In the 'Followers' elegance, you may check out your listing of fanatics in more detail.

Chapter 10: Marketing on LinkedIn

What will make customers mute your posts on one-of-a-kind social media structures and crown you as silly will assist you set up your emblem as an professional on LinkedIn. LinkedIn is the maximum essential B2B community in which publishing press releases and important business enterprise statistics isn't most effective expected however will also get you the right connections and help you grow a a achievement commercial business enterprise.

LinkedIn typically gets a bump particularly due to the reality humans don't actually know a way to use it. Since it is centered round business enterprise organization-related content material fabric and not tour images, many determine to write down this platform off. But sincerely because it appears tougher to connect to human beings on LinkedIn, doesn't recommend is not viable.

If you are a B2B enterprise, then that is the platform you need to definitely invest the most of a while and electricity in. But if you assume that LinkedIn is nothing extra but a network in which interest seekers add their resumes hoping to get hired, you cannot be extra incorrect. LinkedIn can be a beneficial advertising and advertising tool if used the proper manner.

So, don't give up on LinkedIn definitely but if you don't understand what to do collectively along with your corporation page. This financial wreck will train you all there may be to apprehend about marketing and advertising and marketing your enterprise on this platform.

Optimizing Your Page

You can also have created your organisation page on LinkedIn with achievement, but that doesn't suggest that your method may be a success. Your commercial enterprise organisation web web page is the general public listing of your enterprise, every inside the LinkedIn's on-net web page seek, in addition to on Google. In order to make sure that your net web page might be easy-to-discover and at the pinnacle of the hunt results, you can have to optimize it first.

Here are some optimization suggestions for higher standard performance and producing greater leads:

Check Your Company's Info

Check to look if your NAP (call, cope with, and contact variety) is simply everyday with the information on unique listings. By doing so you ensure that human beings can gain you with out problems. This also can sound as too obvious, but you'd be marvel of the harm that a single dot or a incorrect digit can do.

Use the Banner Image

Your banner picture – exceptional at 646 x 220 pixels – may be definitely the element you want to define your emblem and make it really stand out on LinkedIn. Of route, it's far endorsed to live together with your logo's recognition style and shades, but, upload a touch extra price on your LinkedIn goal marketplace. For example, have a few thing like "Become Our Follower to Learn a manner to Manage Your Team" written, a good manner to offer a tempting proposition to the LinkedIn customers.

Use the Link Wisely

Most customers add links on their business web web page that result in their homepage. Don't waste precious space and possibility to direct human beings to a higher touchdown web page and use this danger to capture emails or even ship a custom designed message on your net web page traffic.

Link Your Profile to Your Page

Linking your private LinkedIn profile on your commercial corporation net page may be of great value. Go to your private net web page and click on on on 'Experiences'. Under 'Company Name', upload the decision of your agency.

Don't Shy Away from Keywords

Just like with every different social platform, the usage of relevant key phrases is likewise crucial for your advertising technique on LinkedIn. Make awesome to use the right phrases which might be relevant for your commercial enterprise at a few stage within the net web page, but pay close to hobby to how you're the use of them for your 'About' section.

Have Your Employees on Board

Nothing screams healthful enterprise like having content material fabric cloth employees. Make sure to encourage your team not best to love your company enterprise's LinkedIn net web page however also to percentage your content material material. There are not any better logo ambassadors than the people which might be employed via the enterprise.

Promoting and Selling on LinkedIn

If you need to focus on initiatives or special merchandise on LinkedIn, there may be no better way to do it than via using display off pages. Showcase pages are, in a manner, much like your company net internet page. They are stand-by myself pages in which you can make your massive announcements and introduce humans collectively with your most up to date product launches or offerings, announce unique events, or each extraordinary form of possibility that your enterprise might also moreover furthermore gain from. Think of a exhibit internet web page as a treasured addition for your commercial enterprise business enterprise internet web page in which you could proportion a specific a part of your business organization and engage collectively together along with your target market.

For example, in case your commercial enterprise organization has multiple smaller manufacturers, you can use exhibit pages and create a unique location for each of your manufacturers. Something like Facebook Groups, however in a miles more specific, commercial enterprise enterprise-associated manner.

Businesses use show off pages because of the truth they can:

Share Info about Their Brand. Unlike writing a short repute replace, display off pages make it feasible for you to percent as an entire lot as facts as you'd need your LinkedIn goal marketplace to be privy to.

Share Info best with Relevant People. People comply with simplest those showcases that in particular involved. For instance, if a person is interested by one thing of your enterprise corporation but no longer in a few detail else that you do, they will maximum likely study remarkable the display off that is relevant to them. This technique that you'll have a extra focused goal marketplace, and which you don't need to promote your logo as heaps as you have to on your employer internet net page.

Increase Engagement. Having many exhibit pages method having many opportunities for establishing communique along aspect your well-knowledgeable LinkedIn target market.

Chapter 11: Creating a Successful Showcase Page

Before even considering developing a Showcase Page, it's far of vital importance that you recognize that Showcase Pages can't be truly unpublished. If you want to delete and absolutely deactivate the internet internet page, you need to touch LinkedIn and ask them to put off it. With that in thoughts, you need to pay close to hobby od why and the way you're growing your display off web web page.

A display off internet page can simplest be created through the administrator of the organization internet page. In order to obtain this, comply with the following steps:

1.Go to your business business enterprise agency page and open the drop-down menu that is determined next to the 'Edit' button. Select 'Create a Showcase Page'.

2.Now, a Showcase Page pop-up window will appear. Click on the 'Get Started' button.

3.Enter the applicable statistics much like the choice of your Showcase Page, and lease an administrator for the web page.

4.Click on 'Create Page'. At this aspect, LinkedIn will display you what your web page will seem like. If you are not happy with the appearance, make some changes. If it seems right, bounce to the subsequent step.

five.Finally, click on the 'Publish' button and you're Showcase Page will skip Live very quickly.

Starting a LinkedIn Group

A LinkedIn Group may be very first-rate out of your commercial business enterprise web page, non-public LinkedIn profile, or possibly your showcase pages. LinkedIn businesses are not approximately selling your logo nor about selling your products. At least now not in the plain sense of the phrase, this is. Groups are approximately having a place to talk approximately positive vicinity of hobby or topics in conjunction with your network, in case you need to broaden your target audience and growth their engagement.

So, you may not be able to promote your offerings there, but thru the usage of studying about your intention marketplace, LinkedIn Groups offer you with the possibility of actually improving the sales approach.

Chapter 12: Why Your Business Needs a LinkedIn Group

If you're wondering whether growing and managing a LinkedIn Group is absolutely really worth your money and time, take a look at those blessings to see simply what you can get out of these groups:

Establishing Expertise - If you're a B2B commercial enterprise proprietor, then a LinkedIn Group can be actually what you want to installation your reputation as being one in all the maximum vital professionals for your employer. By taking a thing in discussions, you get to reveal off along side your information.

Driving Traffic – By putting links that direct to your net internet web page or every different income internet page, you may get the risk to pressure more traffic there.

Expanding Your Reach – By having a fixed wherein you may communicate certain topics with like-minded people, you will effects make new connections.

Understanding Your Community – Since you'll be communicating collectively along with your community, you'll have the threat to find out approximately their questions, problems, mind, and so forth. First hand. This will create a exquisite possibility with the intention to form your content material fabric and your offerings with the reason of attracting new customers.

Sending Weekly Updates – Being the owner of a LinkedIn Group, you can get the danger to deliver weekly messages to absolutely everyone who follows your business agency. This may be a notable way as a manner to ensure that your community is aware of the contemporary enterprise corporation facts, product updates, new occasions, and so on.

Setting Up Your Group

Your LinkedIn business enterprise may be installation in a few minutes. It will not take more than truly a few minutes, and the technique is quite smooth and simple. Just have a take a look at the subsequent steps and you will have one up and jogging very quickly:

1.Find 'Interests' at the pinnacle of your web page, click on on it, and then hit 'Groups' from the drop-down menu. The net page with the Group Highlights will appear.

2.Select 'My Groups' decided at the pinnacle of the internet web page.

3.Find 'Create a Group' inside the left sidebar and click on on it.

4.Now, input all of the applicable facts approximately your group: the call of the employer, description, summary, website URL, and plenty of others. Keep in thoughts that the relevant key phrases play a massive feature here as nicely, so make sure to be engaging and descriptive, but moreover tactical.

five.Next, add your image or log. This is non-obligatory, but quite endorsed.

6.When growing your Group, you may have the option to pick out out whether you want it to be public or not. If you don't want the Group to be public, ensure that 'Unlisted' is checked.

7.Accept the Terms of Service.

eight.Finally, hit the 'Create Group' button.

And that's it. Now, you're a proud owner of a LinkedIn Group.

Standard or Unlisted Group?

There are alternatives for your LinkedIn Group – you may select out it to be vast or unlisted.

In a Standard LinkedIn Group:

- The discussions might be proven in Google's are trying to find outcomes

- The participants of the Group can invite different LinkedIn customers to enroll in

In an Unlisted LinkedIn Group:

- The discussions will no longer be examined in seek engine consequences

- Only the participants of the organisation might be capable of see the discussions

- Only the Group's administrator can invite (and approve) clients to join the organisation

- A padlock icon may be examined to indicated that the employer is unlisted

So, all in all, a large agency is an open, public institution, and an unlisted corporation is closed, private institution. Choosing the right one for your industrial corporation is a few issue that splendid you may do. They each have their experts and cons, however in the long run, all of it comes all the manner right down to what you're searching out.

Chapter 13: LinkedIn as a Content Platform

LinkedIn gives the possibility for you the put up content material in an extended shape. Even if you have (and successfully use) a internet website online or a weblog, publishing longer content fabric on LinkedIn will not simplest help you acquire a greater professional social network, but may even throw many extraordinary advantages your manner:

- Your posts will become seen on your personal profile. This will further sell your emblem as every person who clicks on your expert profile on LinkedIn can be succesful to check out the located up posted with the aid of your emblem.

- People that aren't related for your corporation also can see your publish which creates a big opportunity for logo recognition and developing your target market.

- LinkedIn customers can follow your posted content material, in spite of the truth that they do not choose out to follow you.

- Every one in every of your connections can be notified about the posted publish, which tremendous will boom the possibility that the humans you're related to will see the submit.

- The opportunities for appealing with remarkable professionals are appreciably obtained, as readers can also like and touch upon your posts.

Creating Your First Post

Your publish may be without troubles constituted of your LinkedIn domestic net net web page in just a few steps:

1.Click on 'Home' on the top left corner of your LinkedIn Page.

2.Select 'Write an Article' from the top of your web net page.

3.Enter your name within the name region.

4.In 'Write Here', write (or paste) the content material cloth which you preference to position up.

five.Finally, click on on 'Publish' from the pinnacle proper nook.

Keeping It Professional

Since LinkedIn is a community for career-orientated and expert people, it is best comprehensible which you can not post your content fabric in the equal fashion as you write your Insta captions. When posting on LinkedIn, you need to do it in a expert tone if you need to trap the eye no longer pleasant of your connections however one-of-a-kind LinkedIn individuals as properly.

Here are a few suggestions that will help you write a a success LinkedIn placed up in a professional manner:

Solve Problems. Keep in mind that humans need to understand about what you do so as to clear up some troubles that they are coping with. Make tremendous that your content fabric fabric will answer questions and remedy troubles. Your readers will respect if you guide them and train, now not post fluff.

Give Advice. Many more youthful experts who need to try themselves for your company will apprehend having recommendation from specialists. What are the belongings you need you knew even as you have been beginning out? Share some suggestions and educate.

Keep it Up-to-the-Point. Really prolonged content material fabric fabric makes human beings get bored. Your LinkedIn posts have to be among 500 and 800 terms, so make sure now not to post longer content material cloth.

Respond to Comments. Make sure to reply to each comment. Your readers will recognize that you charge their opinion on the way to most likely inspire them to percent your content fabric.

Be Careful with the Links. Links may be protected for your put up, but great if they'll be a part of the speak and make links. Don't surely drop links right away because it will appearance unprofessional and spammy.

Use Rich Media. Adding a few visible factors on your positioned up will make it an awful lot more attractive. On LinkedIn, it's far allowed to apply pictures, presentation from SlideShare, in addition to embed YouTube movies.

Once your put up is published, don't forget to promote it. Make sure which you percentage a hyperlink in your put up on your different social media systems so as to increase your connections, increase focus, and let your goal marketplace understand that you are constantly strolling on something new.

Tips for Getting More LinkedIn Followers

Getting greater people to like your commercial enterprise enterprise net internet page on LinkedIn can sense like an not possible issue to benefit. But at the same time as attracting new fanatics may be extraordinarily a assignment, it's miles truely possible.

Growing your following on LinkedIn comes down to two topics:

1.Promoting your net internet web page on one of a kind systems

2.Implementing some strategies to draw greater human beings

And on the identical time as the number one factor requires a few dedication and try to your issue, I can really assist you with the latter. Here are the final suggestions that will help you growth the quantity of your LinkedIn lovers:

- Create a badge for your LinkedIn web page on the way to be positioned for your net internet site on-line or weblog. You can use the LinkedIn Plugin Generator because of this https://developer.Linkedin.Com/plugins

- Post frequently. According to LinkedIn, the maximum a achievement pages are those that put up at the least 20 instances a month, so make certain that you replace your network on a everyday foundation.

- Make positive to apply the LinkedIn share buttons along with your posts with the intention to encourage your readers to proportion your content material.

- Share interest possibilities postings on your LinkedIn business organization net page. This is one of the important topics that draws the eye of the LinkedIn individuals, so make sure to take care of that.

- Be informative collectively in conjunction with your posts. The maximum a success posts are those who percentage the superb statistics, so ensure to keep your fans updated with cutting-edge enterprise agency records, product development, upcoming activities, and so on.